Chaucer's Canterbury Pilgrims

Retold by

KATHARINE LEE BATES

Professor of English Literature in Wellesley College

Illustrated by

ANGUS MACDONALL

With color plates by

MILO WINTER

Rand McNally & Company

Chicago *New York*

TO

Wallace

"AND he sent us a train of pilgrims: each with a distinct individuality apart from the pilgrimage, all the way from Southwark and the Tabard Inn, to Canterbury and Becket's shrine: and their laughter comes never to an end, and their talk goes on with the stars, and all the railroads which may intersect the spoilt earth forever, cannot hush the 'tramp, tramp' of their horses' feet."

Mrs. Browning's *Book of the Poets.*

THIS little book attempts to tell the story of the immortal pilgrimage by casting into modern English selected portions of *The Canterbury Tales*, with a few interpolated lines, duly bracketed, of connection and explanation. Certain phrases are simplified and a few difficult allusions dropped, but the paraphrase clings as closely as it may under these limitations to Chaucer's own lines. The three tales that have, in their modernized forms, a recognized place in English literature, are given in the respective versions of Dryden, Wordsworth, and Leigh Hunt. From Dryden's poem a few brief passages, especially such as are without warrant in Chaucer's text, have been omitted, and the division into parts is not the same. The quarrel between the Miller and the Manciple, at Bob-up-and-down, pages 290-95, is given in Leigh Hunt's version.

A LIST OF ILLUSTRATIONS

BESEECHING PARDON

PARDON, Great Poet, that all rudely thus
I echo thy clear voice melodious,
Voice of the Day-Star lilting fresh and sweet
Greeting to Earth and all her pilgrim feet.
Did'st not thyself for Lewis, "little son,"
Whose Latin was "but small," the subtly-spun
Labors of old astrology re-dress
In phrase befitting childhood's simpleness?
Five are the trooping centuries between
Thee and the children of this new demesne
Over the western wave. Not all may climb,
To catch the cadence of thy "ryding rime,"
Fair learning's hill, yet would upon them all
Some glimmer of thy sunny soul might fall,
Hint of the brave old days and figures quaint,
When pilgrims sought the Canterbury saint
Less for his saintship than the merry way.
Grant us to follow after as we may,
Fed on the fragments of thy gentle mirth,
Loving with thee the beauty of the earth.

Chaucer

THE TABARD INN AND THE PILGRIMS

WHEN the sweet showers from skies of April blue
The drought of March have piercèd through and through
And bathed each vein in sap whose silent power
Quickens the bud and nourishes the flower.
When the soft west wind with his fragrant breath
Awakened hath in every wood and heath
The tender shoots and when the blithe young sun
His summer course through heaven hath well begun,
And little birds scarce wait till night is gone
To hail with melody the springing dawn,—
For so the joy of nature pricks the heart,—
Then people long from houses to depart
And go a-journeying for love of God
To far-off shrines whose fame is noised abroad,
And specially from every county's end
Of England men to Canterbury wend
The holy blissful Martyr to adore
Whose help has healed them of the ills they bore.

Once it befell when I, in such a season,
In Southwark at the Tabard lodged, for reason
That from this London inn do travelers start
For Canterbury and, devout of heart,
I too would make the pilgrimage that spring,
Some nine and twenty folk came gathering

Site of the Shrine of St. Thomas, Canterbury Cathedral

Together there, as friendly chance did fall,
And pilgrims of Saint Thomas were they all,
Who on the morrow toward his shrine would ride.

The chambers and the stables were so wide
That there were beds for all and of the best;
And shortly, when the sun had sunk to rest,
So had I spoken with them every one
That I was of their fellowship anon
And promised to rise early and to go
Together with them whitherward you know.

But ne'ertheless, while I have time and space,
Before I further in this story pace,
Methinks 'twere well to tell you all I can
About my fellow-pilgrims man by man,
Both of what worldly rank they seemed to be

And how their very selves appeared to me,
The look of them, the array that they were in,
And at a knight then will I first begin.

There was a Knight, well worthy of the name,
Who from the time when he to manhood came
And rode in armor forth, loved chivalry,
Honor and truth, fair-dealing, courtesy.
Full bravely had he served his king in war,
Fought for our faith in heathen lands afar,
And ever won such honor with his sword
In feasts men placed him highest at the board;
But of his bearing modest as a maid;
He never yet in all his life had said,
To any mortal, word of scorn or spite.
He was a very perfect gentle knight.
But as for his array, his worthiness
Showed in his horses more than in his dress.

Norman Crypt, Canterbury Cathedral

The tunic that he wore was coarse and plain
And from his coat of mail had taken stain,
For he from travel was but lately come
And sought the Saint before he sought his home.

With him there was his son, a gay young Squire.
Love was his song and all his heart's desire.
His locks were curly as if laid in press.
Of twenty year of age he was, I guess.
Well-formed he was and of a goodly height,
Active and strong and valorous in fight,
For thrice already had he wielded lance
In Flanders and the pleasant fields of France,
And borne him well, for such a little space,
In hope to stand within his lady's grace.
With white and red his clothes were broidered so
He seemed a meadow where bright blossoms grow.
Singing he was, or fluting, all the day;
He was as fresh as is the month of May.
Short was his gown, with sleeves both long and wide;
Well could he sit his horse and well could ride.
He could make songs and many a tale recite
And he could tilt and dance and draw and write.
Singing of love beneath the moonlight pale,
He slept no more than doth a nightingale.
Courteous he was, lowly and serviceable,
And carved before his father at the table.

A Yeoman and no retinue beside
They had, for so it pleased the Knight to ride,
A Yeoman clad in coat and hood of green.
A sheaf of peacock-arrows bright and keen

Under his belt he bore in archer's wise.
His shafts were feathered skillfully, to rise
Not over high nor yet to droop too low,
And in his hand he bore a mighty bow.
Face brown with sunburn and the hair close cut,
That head of his was very like a nut.
He knew all woodcraft, wore a leather guard
Upon his arm, a buckler and a sword
On one side, while the other did he grace
With a sharp dagger in a jaunty case.
A silver image of Saint Christopher
Hung on his breast and, like the forester
He was, a hunting-horn set off his dress.

There was likewise a Nun, a Prioress,
Called Madame Eglantine. Her smile was coy;
Her greatest oath was only by Saint Loy,
Who helps the goldsmiths fashion trinkets fine.
Sweetly she sang the services divine
A little through her nose, and French she spoke
Full fluently and like to gentlefolk—
Who are in merry England born and grown,
For French of Paris was to her unknown.
Her ways at table were most fine of all;
Upon her breast she let no morsel fall,
But daintily her strip of bread would dip
Within the broth nor wet her finger-tip,
Nor spill a drop as to her mouth it went.
Upon good manners all her mind was bent.
When the cup passed down the board, she wiped so clean
Her upper lip no spot of grease was seen
Upon the wine when she had drunken, nor

Was there a dish she would be snatching for.
And surely she would put us at our ease
With gracious words and little pleasantries,
And yet took pains that it should well be seen
By these her courtly airs and stately mien
To her was due most reverent respect.
As for her conscience, 'twas no less select.
So pitiful she was, if it should hap
She saw a mouse caught fast within a trap
Her tears would flow, even though its life were fled.
Some little hounds she had and those she fed
On roasted meat and milk and wheaten bread,
And sore she wept if one of them was dead,
Or stroke of pilgrim's staff should make one smart,
For all was conscience, all was tender heart.
Full gracefully her gathered kerchief lay
Upon her modest shoulders; eyes as grey
As glass; a little mouth all red and soft;
A comely nose; a forehead there aloft
Broad as my hand, for truly I must own
Not anyone could call her undergrown.
Her cloak was in the fashion, I divined;
About her arm a rosary was twined
Of coral, with some few green beads that told
The longer prayers and with a brooch of gold,
On which was written first a crownèd A,
And after, *Amor vincit omnia*,
To wit, *Love conquers all.* With her rode on
A Nun—her chaplain—and a Priest, Sir John.

A Monk there was did his profession grace,
A sportsman, whose devotion was the chase;

Green Court Gate, Canterbury Cathedral

A manly man, to be an abbot able;
Full many a dainty horse had he in stable;
And when he rode, men might his bridle hear
Jingling in a whistling wind as clear
And full as loud as doth the chapel bell.
Wherever he held rule o'er convent cell,
The discipline, be sure, was nothing strict,
Like that laid down of old by Benedict.
This monk would let the dull old ways go by
And with the new world walk in jollity.
'Tis writ that hunters are not holy men,
But for that text he would not give a hen.
As for that other text comparing to
Fish out of water monks like this one, who
So often may be met with out of cloister,
He held it, told he me, not worth an oyster,
And I agreed with him that he was wise.
Why should he study and weary out his eyes

Poring on books, or labor himself lean
With spade and hoe, as bade Saint Augustine?
Could his two hands this damaged world repair?
Saints fond of work were welcome to his share.
So on the chase he spurred from dawn till night.

The Monk's Dog

Greyhounds he had, as swift as bird in flight,
For he no cost in horse and hound would spare,
Since all his joy was hunting of the hare.
I saw his sleeves were trimmed above the hand
With rich grey fur, the finest of the land,
And to make fast his hood beneath his chin
He had, well wrought of gold, a curious pin;
There was a love-knot in the larger end.
Glistened like glass his bald pate reverend;

The Monk's Dog

His face shone, too, as if with oil and wine;
He was a right fat lord, this priest divine.
Little there was his quick eyes noted not,
Those eyes that gleamed like coals beneath the pot.
Well-greased his boots, his horse in prime condition,—
A prelate that became his holy mission.
He was not pale, not he, as piteous ghost.
A fat swan loved he best of any roast.
His palfrey was as brown as is a berry.

A Friar there was, vain-glorious and merry.
He had a begging district of his own;
No other in those bounds might beg a bone;
His flattering speech supplied him well with food,
For there is none of all that friar brood,
Whate'er the color of the frock may be,
Can wheedle with so soft a tongue as he.
Although his morals were not much to boast,
He to his Order was a noble post.
Familiar friend he was and gossip dear
Of country gentlemen that make good cheer,—
Franklins we call them,—and of dames discreet
Who chose him for confessor, as was meet;
For well they knew that he would not be hard on
Their pleasant vices but would sweetly pardon.
His penances full easy were and light
If any glint of money was in sight;
When alms unto his Order had been given,
He held it sign the sinner was well shriven;
He would avow that he was not averse
To looking for repentance in the purse,
For many a wight so hard is of his heart

He may not weep, though sore his conscience smart;
So in the stead of tears and prayers men should
Bestow their silver on the Brotherhood.
His hanging cowl was always stuffed with knives
And pins to peddle among pretty wives.
And certainly he had a merry note;
His fiddle matched the music of his throat;
He bore away the palm for minstrelsy;
His neck was white as is the fleur-de-lis;
In wrestling he could throw a champion down;
He knew the taverns well in every town
And every jolly tapster better than
The hungry and the sick. So great a man
As he—though friars were sent to serve the poor—
Should not be seen about the pesthouse door.
It's not respectable, it ill becomes
A personage of mark to haunt the slums;
Far better is it at the rich man's table
To sit and feast and then perchance be able,
In pause between the pasty and the roast,
To coax a goodly present from the host.
No man so meek, so virtuous as he,
And none could equal him in beggary;
For though a widow had not even a shoe,
So lovely was his Latin that it drew
From out her scanty hoard a copper bit.
He lisped a little, when he thought of it,
To make his English sweet upon his tongue,
And in his harping after he had sung,
His eyes would twinkle in his head as bright
As do the stars upon a frosty night.
They called him Father Huberd, it appeared.

Christ Gate, Canterbury

A Merchant was there, with a forkèd beard,
In motley clad, and high on horse he sat,
Upon his head a Flanders beaver hat.
His neatly-buckled boots declared expense;
His views he voiced with much self-consequence,
Forever telling how his commerce throve,
And that the king should let no pirates rove
The English Channel, cost it what it might
To clear the seas and do the merchants right.
So shrewd was he that those who with him met
No whit suspected that he was in debt,
For he full pompously would toss and ring
The foreign coins and drive his bargaining.

He was a worthy man withal, no doubt.
His name I never happened to find out.

A Clerk of Oxford with us journeyèd,
A scholar who loved logic more than bread.
Lean as a rake the horse was that he sat,
And he himself, I warrant, was not fat;
A hollow look he had and sober, too;
A threadbare cape he wore, as scholars do,
For as yet he had no parish, nor would bend
His sacred learning to a worldly end;
For he would rather have at his bed's head
Twenty volumes, bound in black or red,
Of Aristotle and his philosophy
Than garments rich or fiddle or psaltery;
Yet, though philosopher, he did not hold
Their magic stone transforming clay to gold,
But all the money that his friends could spare
He spent on books and learning, while his prayer
Rose ever that in peace the souls of those
Who gave him means to study might repose.
Study was all he cared for, all he heeded;
Not one word spake he further than was needed,
And that was to the purpose, quick and short,
Uttered with dignity, of high import.
Inspiring unto virtue was his speech,
And gladly would he learn and gladly teach.

A Man of Law there was, wary and keen.
The portico of St. Paul's Church had seen
Him often deep in talk with legal folk
Grave was his air and cautiously he spoke;

His words were wondrous wise. When he appeared
Upon the justice-bench the guilty feared.
Of fees, and robes had he full many a one;
So safe a man for titles was there none,

Approach to Cathedral, Mercury Lane, connecting with Christ Gate, Canterbury

And none so busy, yet, for all his buzz,
Methought he seemèd busier than he was.
At tip of tongue he had all judgments down
From old King William, but his chief renown

It was that none could ever pick a flaw
In any will or deed that he might draw;
And every statute could he say by rote.
He rode but simply, in a quiet coat
Whose silken belt was set with bosses small.
Naught more of his array do I recall.

A Franklin rode beside him like his shadow.
His beard was white as daisy in the meadow;
Ruddy his face; well loved he, I divine,
At morningtide a sop of cake in wine;
In joy he lived and would till life were done,
For he was Epicurus' very son,
Greek sire of epicures, whose doctrine ran
That pleasure is the highest good of man.
A householder so liberal was he,
Saint Julian himself he seemed to be—
The hospitable saint whom travelers pray
To send them lodging at the shut of day.
His bread, his ale, ne'er fell below the best;
His stores of wine astonished every guest;
Pasties of meat and fish his board would load
In such abundance that it fairly snowed,
Within that house of his, victual and drink,
And all the dainties that a man could think.
And as the year from moon to moon would wear,
So with the seasons would he change his fare.
Full many a partridge fattened in his mew,
And many a bream and carp his fish pond knew.
Woe to his cook, were dinner late a trice
Or should a poignant sauce be scant of spice.
All day his table spread stood in his hall,

So kept he open house for one and all.
As Justice, to the county-seat he went;
And often had he sat in Parliament.
A dagger and a hawking-pouch of silk
Hung at his girdle, white as morning-milk.
Columns of figures could he sharply scan.
Was nowhere such a worthy gentleman.

There were a Carpenter, Hat-maker, Dyer,
Tapestry-worker, Weaver, in attire
All spick and span, each in the dress decreed
For his own guild, important guilds indeed.
These five were something better than their class;
The law allows to common craftsmen brass
And nothing more for ornament, but on
Their purses, belts, and knives fair silver shone.
Each of them seemed a citizen well fit
Upon his guildhall platform high to sit,
And each, should he go on as he began,
Was in the way to be an alderman;
For these were well-to-do, with sums laid by,
As willingly their wives would testify,
Brisk city-dames who longed, and well they might,
To be called Madame, and to have the right
To walk ahead of neighbors up the aisle,
While servants bore their cloaks in royal style.

A Cook they'd taken with them, one who knew
The art of flavoring a chicken stew
With cypress-root, which some call galingale.
He was a perfect judge of London ale,
And he could roast and seethe and boil and fry,

Well make a chowder and a mutton pie;
But of his gifts was cleanness not the best.

There was a Sailor, hailing from the west—
For aught I know from Dartmouth. On his nag
He rode in sailor fashion, like a bag.
His frock of homely frieze fell to his knee;
A dagger hanging on a cord had he
About his neck under his arm well down;
The summer sun had made his hue all brown.
He was a right good fellow of a sort;
When wine was in his cargo, it fell short,
For while the merchant slept, the skipper drank
His prisoners at sea must walk the plank;
For if he fought and had the upper hand,
By water he sent them home to every land;
His easy conscience let such matters slip;
But there was none his match for seamanship,
To reckon well his currents and his tides,
Harbors and shoals and moon and all besides;
Wary, but bold on course once undertaken;
With many a tempest had his beard been shaken;
He knew his coast from Jutland down to Spain;
The ship he sailed was called the Maudelayne.

A Doctor, one whose fame was nothing dim;
In all the world there was no man like him
To speak of physic and of surgery,
For he was grounded in astronomy;
He would each patient's lucky star disclose,
Nor give him medicine till that star rose;
He knew the cause of every malady

And, summoned to a sick man, he would try,
For first of all, to find the very root
Of the disorder; then one fleet of foot
Would fetch him from his own apothecary
Sirups and drugs, of which he was not chary,
For doctor and apothecary thrive
Each by the other and in gain connive.
He knew all books of healing, African,
Greek, English, Spanish, and Arabian.
As for himself, he looked unto his food,
Nor took too much, but nourishing and good;
That drugs are meant for patients is no libel;
His study was but little on the Bible;
His doctor's robes, crimson and bluish grey,
Well lined with silk, he wore this holiday;
Yet was he thrifty and would hoard the pence
That fell so thick in times of pestilence,
For gold is said to be medicinal;
Therefore his love of gold was natural.

There was a Wife of Bath, that thriving city.
A little deaf she was, the more the pity.
At weaving cloth no Fleming could outdo her;
Not Ghent itself could hold a candle to her.
In all the parish, goodwife was there none
Might pass before her, when some relic-bone
Invited to the altar; if they should,
Her anger threw her out of pious mood.
Of finest weft her kerchiefs; I'll be bound
Those that she wore on Sunday weighed ten pound,
With golden net so richly were they spread.
Her well-tied stockings were of scarlet-red;

Full supple were her riding-boots and new;
Bold was her face, and fair, and red of hue.
A worthy woman she, as husbands five
Might have avouched, were one of them alive.
Thrice had she journeyed to Jerusalem,
In far-off streams had wet her mantle's hem,
To Rome had roamed, a pilgrimage had made
To Our Lady of Boulogne, her vows had paid
To good Saint James of Spain, and by the Rhine
Had seen in proud Cologne the Magi's shrine.

Pilgrims' Flasks

Much did she know of wandering by the way.
Between her teeth were gaps, the sooth to say.
Upon an ambler easily she sat
Well wrapt from wind, and on her head a hat
As broad as is a target or a shield;
A riding-skirt her gala dress concealed;
She rode astride and wore a pair of spurs.
In bantering a lively tongue was hers;

In love-spells and in charms she dealt, perchance,
For of that art she knew the blithe old dance.

A good man in the cleric garb was there,
A village Parson, poor in house and fare,
But rich he was in holy thought and work.
He was withal a learnèd man, a clerk
That would Christ's very gospel truly preach,
And his parishioners devoutly teach.
Benign he was and wondrous diligent,
Full patient in adversity as sent
From God, and he of this had known his share.
Always full loath he was to bring to bear
The curse appointed by the Church on those
Who would not pay his tithes; he rather chose
Out of his pittance to relieve the poor;
In little he could find abundant store.
Wide was his parish, and houses far asunder,
Yet failed he never, not for rain nor thunder,
To visit in their sickness and their woe
The farthest in his parish, high and low,
Upon his feet, a staff within his hand.
By this example all might understand
God's will should first be done and then be taught.
This rule of life he from the gospel brought;
A figure of his own he put thereto,—
That if gold rust, then what shall iron do?
For if a priest take stain, in whom we trust,
What wonder is it that a layman rust?
Let priests beware and note the shame is deep
Of spotted shepherd by a spotless sheep.
Well ought a priest example pure to give

The Baptistery, Canterbury Cathedral

By his own cleanness how his flock should live.
He did not let his parish out for hire,
Leaving his sheep to fall into the mire,
That he might enter on the London race
For wealth and comfort and exalted place,

Or in an abbey at his ease to mould,
But dwelt at home and guarded well his fold,
So that the wolf e'er found him ware and wary;
He was a shepherd and no mercenary.
But though he lived in holy righteousness,
To sinful man he was not pitiless,
Nor sharp of speech nor easily indignant,
But in his teaching gracious and benignant.
To draw folk on to heaven by showing fair
A good example was his daily care;
But were there any person obstinate,
Whether of lowly or of high estate,
Fearless and keen would his rebuke be hurled.
No better priest, I trow, is in the world.
He did not covet pomp, he did not spice
A simple conscience with distinctions nice.
The lore of Christ, for love and not for pelf
He taught, but first he followed it himself.

With him a Ploughman rode, his brother, who
Had tilled the fields full many a season through,
An honest toiler, good to delve and haul,
Living in peace and charity with all.
God ever loved he best, with all his heart,
Though gain or loss fell to his humble part;
Then even as himself he loved his neighbor,
Would thresh, would dig, or whatsoever labor
Was needed, he would give, for Christ's dear sake,
To any one hard pressed, nor wages take,
If so he could, for well his tithes he paid,
And poor he was, as garb and steed betrayed;
In peasant-smock he rode upon a mare.

A Steward and a Miller cantered there,
A Summoner, a Pardoner, these four,
A Manciple and I; there were no more.

The Miller was a sturdy churl to see;
Full big of muscle and of bone was he;
The wrestling matches proved his strength no sham,
For everywhere he took the prize, a ram.
He was short-shouldered, broad, a thick-set clown,
Could run against a door and break it down
Or heave it off the hinges with his head.
That beard of his as any fox was red,
And for a spade its shape would not be bad.
On the tip end of his nose a wart he had
Topped with a tuft of hairs as red, I vow,
As are the coarse ear-bristles of a sow;
As for his nostrils, they were black and wide.
A sword and buckler bare he by his side.
His mouth was like a furnace and full soon
Began to belch foul stories. A buffoon
He was, whose jestings savored all of sin.
Thrice would he take his toll of corn, yet in
Much feel of falling grain the rogue had come
To have for honest skill a golden thumb;
So good a miller had no need to steal.
His coat was white, as powdered still with meal,
But with a sky-blue hood of fashion gay
He had done honor to the holiday.
His bagpipe brought our pilgrimage renown,
For lustily he piped us out of town.

A Manciple there was of civil sort,
Who bought provisions for an Inn of Court—
A house where lawyers lodge—and caterers well
Might learn of him how best to buy and sell.
Cash down or credit, wine or meat or bread,
He managed so that he came out ahead.
Now is not that of God a full fair grace
That such a plain man's wit should so outpace
The wisdom of a heap of learnèd men?
Of masters had he more than three times ten
Deep versed in law, expert at legal writ.
There were a dozen in that house right fit
To act as stewards for the land and rent
Of any lord in England's wide extent,
Enabling him to live, were he not mad,
In honor, free from debt, on what he had,
Or increase his wealth by limiting his bounty,—
Men who could do the business of a county
And guide it through what perils might befall;
And yet this Manciple hoodwinked them all.

The Steward was a slender, choleric man.
His beard was shaved upon a thrifty plan;
Round his bald top, like that of tonsured priest,
The fringe of close-cut hair was of the least.
His legs were long and lean, like to a staff;
There was no sign upon them of a calf.
Of wheat and corn he garnered good amounts
No flaw was ever found in his accounts.
Well knew he what in drought and what in rain
Should be the yielding of his seed and grain.
His lord's full stock, sheep, horses, cattle, swine,

His stores, his dairy, poultry yard,—in fine,
All that he had lay in this Steward's hand.
His lordship, since he came of age, had scanned
The reckonings year by year nor could he find
That anywhere the estate had run behind.
No hind nor herdsman could in any wise
Throw dust in this sharp Steward's sleepless eyes,
But like the pestilence they dreaded him.
The shadow of full many a green-leaved limb
Fell on his home, fair set on level sward,
For he could purchase better than his lord.
From the wealth that he had privily put by
He would lend unto his lord, who guilelessly,
Not weeting 'twas his own already, would
Add to his thanks a costly coat and hood.
The Steward in his youth had learned the trade
Of carpenter, nor had his skill decayed.
He rode a good gray cob, whose name was Scot;
Its coat was dappled with full many a spot.
In dull-blue surcoat he the journey made,
And by his side he bare a rusty blade.
Of Norfolk was this man of whom I tell;
He lived hard by the town of Baldeswell.
With coat tucked up about him, friar-mode,
The hindermost of all our troop he rode.

A Summoner— who men of ill report
Summons before the Church's special court—
Was with us. Children feared to look on him,
His face, as red as painted cherubim,
So hideous was with whelkes and blotches, sign
He loved too well strong food and stronger wine.

When drunk, as oft he was from eve to matin,
Then would he speak no syllable but Latin;
Brief phrases had the fellow, two or three,
Over and over heard from some decree
Read in the Court he haunted every day:
And well ye know, a parrot or a jay
Can cry out "Watt" as well as can the Pope;
But 'twere in vain within his mind to grope
For further learning than this echo-cry
In which was spent all his philosophy.
He was an easy-going rascal, too;
For a quart of wine he would forbear to do
His office, glad to let offenders sink
Their souls in sin, so long as he might drink.
Sly hand at plucking pigeons, oft he used
To frighten folk who had not been accused
And take a bribe for letting them go free.
A flaring garland on his head had he
Big as the hoop set on a tavern-stake.
A buckler had he made him of a cake.

With him a Pardoner rode,—twin spirits these,—
A seller of the Pope's indulgences,
But just returned from pilgrimage to Rome.
Full loud he sang: "Come hither, Sweetheart, come!"
The Summoner roared the bass; was never found
A trumpet that had half so great a sound.
This Pardoner had hair as yellow as wax,
But smooth it hung, as doth a hank of flax;
His locks drooped one by one adown his head,
So long that they his shoulders overspread;
All thin and sleek upon his gown they lay.

For jollity, his hood he had packed away.
And so, with dangling tresses, mile on mile
He rode in what he deemed the latest style;
Save for a little cap, his head was bare.
He had the glaring eyeballs of a hare.
A picture of our Lord was on his cap.
His wallet lay before him on his lap,
Brimful of pardons come from Rome all hot.
His voice was small as any goat's, and not
A sign of beard he had; there could not be
A better cheat and Pardoner than he;
A pillowcase he would have had us hail—
So much a kiss—as the Madonna's veil;
A shred he showed us of St. Peter's sail
Spread on that day which saw his courage fail,
Walking the sea; a brass cross set with stones
He had, and in glass cases, "pigges bones."
With precious relics such as these, he fooled
The simple country-folk, devout, unschooled,
And got more money from them in a day
Than in two months they to the Parson pay;
And thus with flattery and lies he made
These rustics dance to any tune he played.
But yet, though many a vice his life might smirch,
He was a noble preacher in the church.
Well could he read a lesson or a story,
But best of all he sang an offertory;
For well he knew, after that song was done,
That he must preach and polish up his tongue
To gather in the silver from the crowd;
Therefore he sang so merrily and loud.

Now have I told you briefly, as I planned,
The rank, equipment, number of our band,
And why assembled was this company
In Southwark, at this gentle hostelry
That's called The Tabard, close beside The Bell.

The Tabard Inn

But now it is high time that I should tell
How on that night, when at the tavern door
Dismounted had we all, ourselves we bore.
Then to narrate our journey I engage
And all the adventures of our pilgrimage;
But I must pray you to forgive it me,
If I have not set folk in their degree,
Here in this tale, as each man ought to be.
My wit is short, and that ye well may see.

Our Host warm welcome gave us every one
And down to supper set he us anon

And served us with the best of wine and food
For which our pilgrim appetites were good.
A seemly man our landlord was withal,
Fit to be marshal in baronial hall;
A portly man he was, with dancing eyes;
No better citizen in London; wise,
Ready of speech, in courtesy not slack;
Nothing that makes for manhood did he lack.
He had a merry heart, with all the rest,
And after supper he began to jest,
And told of pastimes among other things.
As soon as we had paid our reckonings,
Thus spake he: "Gentles all, upon my word
Right welcome are ye; let the truth be heard
And let me say I have not seen this year
So blithe a company assembled here.
I fain would give you pleasure, wist I what,
And now there comes to me a mirthful plot
To make your pilgrimage with frolic fraught
And, by my faith, the same shall cost you naught.
Ye go to Canterbury; God you speed!
The blissful Martyr help you in your need!
And well I wot ye would beguile the way
With telling tales and making holiday.
For how, in sooth, for sin should it atone
To ride along as dumb as any stone?
Leave it to me, and I will make you glad;
In penance still is comfort to be had.
Now if it please you all, by way of fun,
To carry out this sport my wits have spun,
And promise to perform what I shall say,
To-morrow, as ye ride along the way,

The Transept of the Martyrdom, Canterbury Cathedral

Then, by my father's soul, if ye should grieve,
Ye may cut off my head,— I give you leave.
Hold up your hands and trust the rest to me."
We were not long in coming to agree;
'Twas not a case for serious debate;
We laughed and bid him let us know our fate,
Assuring him he should have all his will.

"Gentles," quoth he, "take not my boldness ill,
Nor mar my mirthful meaning with disdain.
This is the point, to speak it brief and plain.
The Canterbury road to shorten, you
Shall each relate in going stories two
And on the homeward journeying two more,—
Stories of what befell in days of yore,
And he who, when again within this hall

Ye gather, shall have borne him best of all,
That is to say, hath told for our content
Tales of best wisdom and most merriment,
Shall have a supper, at our common cost,
Here in this room, sirs, sitting by this post,
The night we come again from Canterbury;
And, by your leave, to make you all more merry,
Will I myself full gladly with you ride,
At my own charges, and will be your guide,
And whoso dare my judgment once gainsay
Shall pay our full expenses by the way.
Now if ye all vouchsafe that it be so,
Tell me at once—let further talking go—
And I'll arrange to lead you on the morn."

This thing was granted and our oaths were sworn
With jocund heart; a fuller grace to show,
We prayed him of his courtesy to go,
And begged him be our governor and sit
In judgment on our tales and, as was fit,
Provide the supper—at a certain price—
And we would all fall in with his device
And do his bidding. Thus without demur
We made our host our wayside arbiter.
And thereupon the wine-cup went around;
We drank, and then our sleeping places found
Without more tarrying, for with the dawn
The Canterbury Pilgrims must be gone.

The Pilgrims' Way from London

THE FIRST DAY

When in the east the day began to spring,
Uprose our Host from his short slumbering,
And woke us like the early-crowing cock,
And gathered us together in a flock,
And forth we rode, two miles at easy pace,
To the brook that's called St. Thomas' Watering-place.
And there our Host reined in his horse and quoth:
"Gentles, so please you, well ye know your oath,
And here I charge you keep your plighted word.
If even-song and matin-song accord,
Let see now who shall tell the opening tale.
As ever I hope to drink of wine or ale,
He that rebels against my rule shall pay

The costs of all of us upon the way.
Now draw ye cut, before we journey hence,
And he who hath the shortest shall commence."
[And from the dewy hedgerow, while he spoke,
A twig he plucked that into bits he broke,
Hiding the uneven ends within his hand,
And ran his eye along our pilgrim band.]
"Sir Knight, my master and my lord," quoth he,
"Ride up and draw, for that is my decree.
Come near," quoth he, "my Lady Prioress,
And ye, Sir Clerk, put by your bashfulness,
And ponder not; but to it, every man."
Forthwith to draw each one of us began,
And whether so it chanced or so was planned,
Whether by lot or luck or sleight of hand,
The sooth is this, the cut fell to the Knight,
Of which full blithe and glad was every wight;
And tell he must his tale, as was but right,
By promise and agreement overnight,
As ye have heard. Why say what all folk know?
And when this good man saw that it was so,
As one that wise was and obedient
To keep a promise made with free assent,
He said: "Since I am to begin the game,
Welcome the cut, in good Saint Thomas' name!
Now let us ride and hearken what I say."
And with that word we rode upon our way,
And merrily began he to unfold
His tale anon, and this is what he told:

"Now let us ride and hearken what I say"

The Knight

THE KNIGHT'S TALE

PRELUDE

In days of old there lived, of mighty fame,
A valiant prince; and Theseus was his name:
A chief who more in feats of arms excelled
The rising nor the setting sun beheld:
Of Athens he was lord; much land he won,

And added foreign countries to his crown:
In Scythia with the warrior-queen he strove,
Whom first by force he conquered, then by love;
He brought in triumph back the beauteous dame,
With whom her sister, fair Emilia, came.
With honor to his home let Theseus ride,
With love to friend, and fortune for his guide,
And his victorious army at his side.
I pass their warlike pomp, their proud array,
Their shouts, their songs, their welcome on the way:
But were it not too long, I would recite
The feats of Amazons, the fatal fight
Betwixt the hardy queen and hero knight;
The town besieged, and how much blood it cost
The female army and the Athenian host;
The spousals of Hippolita the queen;
What tilts and tourneys at the feast were seen;
The storm at their return, the ladies' fear:—
But these and other things I must forbear.

The field is spacious I design to sow,
With oxen far unfit to draw the plough:
The remnant of my tale is of a length
To tire your patience, and to waste my strength;
And trivial accidents shall be forborne,
That others may have time to take their turn;
As was at first enjoined us by mine host:
That he whose tale is best, and pleases most,
Should win his supper at our common cost.

And therefore where I left I will pursue
This ancient story, whether false or true,

In hope it may be mended with a new.
The prince I mentioned, full of high renown,
In this array drew near the Athenian town;
When in his pomp, and utmost of his pride,
Marching, he chanced to cast his eye aside,
And saw a choir of mourning dames, who lay
By two and two across the common way:
At his approach they raised a rueful cry
And beat their breasts, and held their hands on high,
Creeping and crying, till they seized at last
His courser's bridle, and his feet embraced.

"Tell me," said Theseus, "what and whence you are,
And why this funeral pageant you prepare?
Is this the welcome of my worthy deeds
To meet my triumph in ill-omened weeds?
Or envy you my praise, and would destroy
With grief my pleasures, and pollute my joy?
Or are you injured, and demand relief?
Name your request, and I will ease your grief."

The most in years of all the mourning train
Began, but swoonèd first away for pain;
Then scarce recovered, spoke: "Nor envy we
Thy great renown, nor grudge thy victory;
'Tis thine, O king! the afflicted to redress,
And fame has filled the world with thy success:
We, wretched women, sue for that alone
Which of thy goodness is refused to none:
Let fall some drops of pity on our grief,
If what we beg be just and we deserve relief:
For none of us, who now thy grace implore,

But held the rank of sovereign queen before;
Till, thanks to giddy Chance, which never bears
That mortal bliss should last for length of years,
She cast us headlong from our high estate,
And here in hope of thy return we wait;
And long have waited in the temple nigh
Built to the gracious goddess Clemency.
But reverence thou the Power whose name it bears,
Relieve the oppressed, and wipe the widow's tears;
I, wretched I, have other fortune seen,
The wife of Capaneus, and once a queen:
At Thebes he fell; cursed be the fatal day!
And all the rest thou seest in this array,
To make their moan, their lords in battle lost
Before that town besieged by our confederate host:
But Creon, old and impious, who commands
The Theban city, and usurps the lands,
Denies the rite of funeral fires to those
Whose breathless bodies yet he calls his foes.
Unburned, unburied, on a heap they lie;
Such is their fate, and such his tyranny;
No friend has leave to bear away the dead
But with their lifeless limbs his hounds are fed."
At this she shrieked aloud; the mournful train
Echoed her grief, and groveling on the plain
With groans, and hands upheld, to move his mind,
Besought his pity to their helpless kind.

The prince was touched, his tears began to flow,
And, as his tender heart would break in two,
He sighed; and could not but their fate deplore,
So wretched now, so fortunate before.

Then lightly from his lofty steed he flew,
And raising one by one the suppliant crew,
To comfort each full solemnly he swore,
That by the faith which knights to knighthood bore,
And whate'er else to chivalry belongs,
He would not cease, till he revenged their wrongs;
That Greece should see performed what he declared;
And cruel Creon find his just reward.
He said no more, but, shunning all delay,
Rode on; nor entered Athens on his way:
But left his sister and his queen behind;
And waved his royal banner in the wind;
Where in an argent field the god of war
Was drawn triumphant on his iron car;
Red was his sword, and shield, and whole attire,
And all the godhead seemed to glow with fire;
E'en the ground glittered where the standard flew,
And the green grass was dyed to sanguine hue.
High on his pointed lance his pennon bore
His Cretan fight, the conquered Minotaur:
The soldiers shout around with generous rage,
And in that victory their own presage.
He praised their ardor: inly pleased to see
His host the flower of Grecian chivalry.
All day he marched, and all the ensuing night,
And saw the city with returning light.
The process of the war I need not tell,—
How Theseus conquered, and how Creon fell:
Or after, how by storm the walls were won,
Or how the victor sacked and burned the town:
How to the ladies he restored again
The bodies of their lords in battle slain:

And with what ancient rites they were interred;
All these to fitter time shall be deferred.
I spare the widows' tears, their woeful cries,
And howling at their husbands' obsequies;
How Theseus at these funerals did assist,
And with what gifts the mourning dames dismissed.

Thus when the victor-chief had Creon slain,
And conquered Thebes, he pitched upon the plain
His mighty camp, and, when the day returned,
The country wasted, and the hamlets burned;
And left the pillagers, to rapine bred,
Without control to strip and spoil the dead.

There, in a heap of slain, among the rest
Two youthful knights they found beneath a load oppressed
Of slaughtered foes, whom first to death they sent,
The trophies of their strength, a bloody monument.
Both fair, and both of royal blood they seemed,
Whom kinsmen to the crown the heralds deemed;
That day in equal arms they fought for fame;
Their swords, their shields, their surcoats were the same.
Close by each other laid they pressed the ground;
Their manly bosoms pierced with many a grisly wound;
Nor well alive nor wholly dead they were,
But some faint signs of feeble life appear:
The wandering breath was on the wing to part,
Weak was the pulse, and hardly heaved the heart.
These two were sisters' sons; and Arcite one,
Much famed in fields, with valiant Palamon.

From these their costly arms the spoilers rent,
And softly both conveyed to Theseus' tent;
Whom known of Creon's line, and cured with care,
He to his city sent as prisoners of the war.
Hopeless of ransom, and condemned to lie
In durance, doomed a lingering death to die.

This done, he marched away with warlike sound,
And to his Athens turned, with laurels crowned,
Where happy long he lived, much loved, and more re-
nowned.
But in a tower, and never to be loosed,
The woeful captive kinsmen are enclosed.

Towers of the West Gate, Canterbury

PART I

Thus year by year they pass, and day by day,
Till once ('twas on the morn of cheerful May)
The young Emilia, fairer to be seen
Than the fair lily on the flowery green,
More fresh than May herself in blossoms new
(For with the rosy color strove her hue)
Waked, as her custom was, before the day,
To do the observance due to sprightly May;
For sprightly May commands our youth to keep
The vigils of her night, and break their sluggard sleep.
In this remembrance Emily ere day
Arose, and dressed herself in rich array;
Fresh as the month, and as the morning fair:
Adown her shoulders fell her length of hair:
A ribbon did the braided tresses bind;
The rest was loose, and wantoned[1] in the wind.
Aurora had but newly chased the night,
And purpled o'er the sky with blushing light,
When to the garden-walk she took her way,
To sport and trip along in cool of day,
And offer maiden vows in honor of the May.

At every turn she made a little stand,
And thrust among the thorns her lily hand
To draw the rose, and every rose she drew
She shook the stalk, and brushed away the dew:
Then parti-colored flowers of white and red
She wove, to make a garland for her head:

1 Played.

This done, she sung and caroled out so clear,
That men and angels might rejoice to hear.
The tower, of which before was mention made,
Within whose keep the captive knights were laid,
Built of a large extent, and strong withal,
Was one partition of the palace wall:
The garden was enclosed within the square,
Where young Emilia took the morning air.
It happened, Palamon, the prisoner knight,
Restless for woe, arose before the light,
And with his jailer's leave desired to breathe
An air more wholesome than the damps beneath.
This granted, to the tower he took his way,
Cheered with the promise of a glorious day:
Then cast a languishing regard around,
And saw with hateful[1] eyes the temples crowned
With golden spires, and all the hostile ground.
He sighed, and turned his eyes, because he knew
'Twas but a larger jail he had in view:
Then looked below, and from the castle's height
Beheld a nearer and more pleasing sight:
The garden, which before he had not seen,
In Spring's new livery clad of white and green,
Fresh flowers in wide parterres, and shady walks
    between.
This viewed, but not enjoyed, with arms across
He stood, reflecting on his country's loss;
Himself an object of the public scorn,
And often wished he never had been born.
At last (for so his destiny required)
With walking giddy, and with thinking tired,
He through a little window cast his sight,

[1] Full of hate.

Though thick of bars, that gave a scanty light:
But even that glimmering served him to descry
The inevitable charms of Emily.
Scarce had he seen, but seized with sudden smart,
Stung to the quick, he felt it at his heart;
Struck blind with overpowering light he stood,
Then started back amazed, and cried aloud.

Young Arcite heard; and up he ran with haste
To help his friend, and in his arms embraced;
And asked him why he looked so deadly wan,
And whence and how his change of cheer began?
Or who had done the offense? "But if," said he,
"Your grief alone is hard captivity;
For love of Heaven with patience undergo
A cureless ill, since fate will have it so:
So stood our horoscope[1] in chains to lie,
And Saturn, in the dungeon of the sky,
Or other baleful aspect,[2] ruled our birth,
When all the friendly stars were under earth:
Whate'er betides, by destiny 'tis done,
And better bear like men, than vainly seek to shun."
"Nor of my bonds," said Palamon again,
"Nor of unhappy[3] planets I complain;
But when my mortal anguish caused my cry,
That moment I was hurt through either eye;
Pierced with a random shaft, I faint away,
And perish with insensible decay:
A glance of some new goddess gave the wound,
Whom, like Actaeon, unaware I found.
Look how she walks along yon shady space,
Not Juno moves with more majestic grace;

---

1 Destiny as foretold by the stars.
2 Other planet in unfavorable position.
3 Unlucky.

And all the Cyprian Queen is in her face.
If thou art Venus (for thy charms confess
That face was formed in Heaven), nor art thou less;
Disguised in habit, undisguised in shape,
O help us captives from our chains to 'scape!
But if our doom be pass'd in bonds to lie
For life, and in a loathsome dungeon die,
Then be thy wrath appeased with our disgrace,
And show compassion to the Theban race,
Oppressed by tyrant power!" While yet he spoke,
Arcite on Emily had fixed his look;
The fatal dart a ready passage found,
And deep within his heart infixed the wound:
So that if Palamon were wounded sore,
Arcite was hurt as much as he or more:
Then from his inmost soul he sighed, and said,
"The beauty I behold has struck me dead:
Unknowingly she strikes, and kills by chance,
Poison is in her eyes, and death in every glance.
Oh! I must ask; nor ask alone, but move
Her mind to mercy, or must die for love!"

Thus Arcite: and thus Palamon replies,
(Eager his tone, and ardent were his eyes:)
"Speak'st thou in earnest, or in jesting vein?"
"Jesting," said Arcite, "suits but ill with pain."
"It suits far worse," said Palamon again,
And bent his brows, "with men who honor weigh,
Their faith to break, their friendship to betray;
But worst with thee, of noble lineage born,
My kinsman, and in arms my br^ther sworn.
Have we not plighted each our holy oath,

That one should be the common good of both?
One soul should both inspire, and neither prove
His fellow's hindrance in pursuit of love?
To this before the gods we gave our hands,
And nothing but our death can break the bands.
This binds thee, then, to further my design;
As I am bound by vow to further thine:
Nor can'st, nor dar'st thou, traitor, on the plain
Appeach my honor, or thine own maintain;
Since thou art of my council, and the friend
Whose faith I trust and on whose care depend:
And wouldst thou court my lady's love, which I
Much rather than release would choose to die?
But thou, false Arcite, never shalt obtain
Thy bad pretence; I told thee first my pain:
For first my love began ere thine was born;
Thou, as my council, and my brother sworn,
Art bound to assist my eldership of right,
Or justly to be deemed a perjured knight."
Thus Palamon. But Arcite with disdain
In haughty language thus replied again:
"Forsworn thyself: the traitor's odious name
I first return, and then disprove thy claim.
If love be passion, and that passion nursed
With strong desires, I loved the lady first.
Can'st thou pretend desire, whom zeal inflamed
To worship, and a power celestial named?
Thine was devotion to the blest above,
I saw the woman, and desired her love;
First owned my passion, and to thee commend
The important secret, as my chosen friend.
Suppose (which yet I grant not) thy desire

A moment elder than my rival fire;
Can chance of seeing first thy title prove?
And know'st thou not, no law is made for love?
Law is to things which to free choice relate;
Love is not in our choice, but in our fate;
Laws are but positive: Love's power, we see,
Is Nature's sanction, and her first decree.
Each day we break the bond of human laws
For Love, and vindicate the common cause.
Laws for defense of civil rights are placed,
Love throws the fences down, and makes a general waste:
Maids, widows, wives, without distinction fall;
The sweeping deluge, Love, comes on and covers all.
If then the laws of friendship I transgress,
I keep the greater, while I break the less;
And both are mad alike, since neither can possess.
Both hopeless to be ransomed, never more
To see the sun, but as he passes o'er.
So thou, if fortune will thy suit advance,
Love on; nor envy me my equal chance:
For I must love, and am resolved to try
My fate, or, failing in the adventure, die!"

Great was their strife, which hourly was renewed,
Till each with mortal hate his rival viewed:
Now friends no more, nor walking hand in hand;
But when they met, they made a surly stand;
And glared like angry lions as they passed,
And wished that every look might be their last.

It chanced at length Pirithous came, to attend
This worthy Theseus, his familiar friend:
Their love in early infancy began
And rose as childhood ripened into man.
Companions of the war; and loved so well,
That when one died, as ancient stories tell,
His fellow, to redeem him, went to hell.

But to pursue my tale; to welcome home
His warlike brother is Pirithous come:
Arcite of Thebes was known in arms long since,
And honored by this young Thessalian prince.
Theseus, to gratify his friend and guest,
Who made our Arcite's freedom his request,
Restored to liberty the captive knight,
But on these hard conditions I recite:
That if hereafter Arcite should be found
Within the compass of Athenian ground,
By day or night, or on whate'er pretence,
His head should pay the forfeit of the offense.
To this, Pirithous, for his friend, agreed,
And on his promise was the prisoner freed.

Unpleased and pensive, hence he takes his way,
At his own peril; for his life must pay.
"What have I gained," he said, "in prison pent,
If I but change my bonds for banishment?
And banished from her sight, I suffer more
In freedom, than I felt in bonds before;
Forced from her presence, and condemned to live:
Unwelcome freedom, and unthanked reprieve:
Heaven is not but where Emily abides,

And where she's absent, all is hell besides.
Next to my day of birth, was that accurst
Which bound my friendship to Pirithous first:
Had I not known that prince, I still had been
In bondage, and had still Emilia seen:
For though I never can her grace deserve,
'Tis recompense enough to see and serve.
O Palamon, my kinsman and my friend,
How much more happy fates thy love attend!
Thine is the adventure; thine the victory:
Well has thy fortune turned the dice for thee:
Thou on that angel's face may'st feed thine
eyes,
In prison, no; but blissful Paradise!
Thou daily see'st that sun of beauty shine,
And lov'st at least in love's extremest line.
I mourn in absence, love's eternal night:
And who can tell but since thou hast her sight,
And art a comely, young, and valiant knight,
Fortune (a various power) may cease to
frown,
And by some ways unknown thy wishes crown?
But I, the most forlorn of human kind,
Nor help can hope, nor remedy can find;
But doomed to drag my loathsome life in care,
For my reward, must end it in despair.
Fire, water, air, and earth, and force of Fates
That governs all, and Heaven that all creates,
Nor art, nor Nature's hand can ease my grief;
Nothing but death, the wretch's last relief:
Then farewell youth, and all the joys that dwell
With youth and life, and life itself—farewell!

"But why, alas! do mortal men in vain
Of fortune, fate, or Providence complain?
God gives us what he knows our wants require,
And better things than those which we desire:
Some pray for riches; riches they obtain;
But watched by robbers, for their wealth are slain:
Some pray from prison to be freed; and come,
When guilty of their vows,[1] to fall at home,
Murdered by those they trusted with their life,
A favored servant, or a bosom wife.
Such dear-bought blessings happen every day,
Because we know not for what things to pray;
Like drunken sots about the streets we roam:
Well knows the sot he has a certain home,
Yet knows not how to find the uncertain place,
And blunders on, and staggers every pace.
Thus all seek happiness; but few can find,
For far the greater part of men are blind.
This is my case, who thought our utmost good
Was in one word of freedom understood:
The fatal blessing came: from prison free,
I starve abroad, and lose the sight of Emily!"

Thus Arcite; but if Arcite thus deplore
His sufferings, Palamon yet suffers more.
For when he knew his rival freed and gone,
He swells with wrath; he makes outrageous moan:
He frets, he fumes, he stares, he stamps the ground;
The hollow tower with clamors rings around:
With briny tears he bathed his fettered feet,
And dropped all o'er with agony of sweat.
"Alas!" he cried, "I wretch in prison pine,

1 When their presumptuous prayers have been granted.

Too happy rival, while the fruit is thine:
Thou liv'st at large, thou draw'st thy native air,
Pleased with thy freedom, proud of my despair:
Thou may'st, since thou hast youth and courage joined,
A sweet behavior, and a solid mind,
Assemble ours, and all the Theban race,
To vindicate on Athens thy disgrace:
And after (by some treaty made) possess
Fair Emily, the pledge of lasting peace:
So thine shall be the beauteous prize; while I
Must languish in despair, in prison die.
Thus all the advantage of the strife is thine,
Thy portion double joys, and double sorrows mine."

The rage of jealousy then fired his soul,
And his face kindled like a burning coal:
Now cold despair, succeeding in her stead,
To livid paleness turns the glowing red.
His blood, scarce liquid, creeps within his veins,
Like water which the freezing wind constrains.
Then thus he said: "Eternal Deities,
Who rule the world with absolute decrees,
And write whatever time shall bring to pass,
With pens of adamant on plates of brass;
What is the race of human kind your care,
Beyond what all his fellow creatures are?
He with the rest is liable to pain;
And like the sheep, his brother beast, is slain.
Cold, hunger, prisons, ills without a cure,
All these he must, and guiltless oft, endure:
Or does your justice, power, or prescience fail,
When the good suffer, and the bad prevail?

What worse to wretched virtue could befall,
If fate or giddy fortune governed all?
Nay, worse than other beasts is our estate;
Them, to pursue their pleasures, you create:
We, bound by harder laws, must curb our will,
And your commands, not our desires, fulfill;
Then when the creature is unjustly slain,
Yet after death, at least, he feels no pain;
But man, in life surcharged with woe before,
Not freed when dead, is doomed to suffer more.
A serpent shoots his sting at unaware;
An ambushed thief forelays a traveler:
The man lies murdered, while the thief and snake,
One gains the thickets, and one thrids[1] the brake.
This let divines decide; but well I know,
Just, or unjust, I have my share of woe,
Through Saturn, seated in a luckless place,
And Juno's wrath, that persecutes my race."

PART II

Let Palamon oppressed in bondage mourn,
While to his exiled rival we return.
By this the sun, declining from his height,
The day had shortened to prolong the night;
The lengthened night gave length of misery
Both to the captive lover and the free.
For Palamon in endless prison mourns,
And Arcite forfeits life if he returns.
The banished never hopes his love to see,
Nor hopes the captive lord his liberty.
'Tis hard to say who suffers greater pains;

[1] Threads.

One sees his love, but cannot break his chains;
One free, and all his motions uncontrolled,
Beholds whate'er he would, but what he would behold.
Judge as you please, for I will haste to tell
What fortune to the banished knight befell.—
When Arcite was to Thebes returned again,
The loss of her he loved renewed his pain;
His eyeballs in their hollow sockets sink,
Bereft of sleep, he loathes his meat and drink.
He withers at his heart, and looks as wan
As the pale specter of a murdered man;
That pale turns yellow, and his face receives
The faded hue of sapless boxen leaves:
In solitary groves he makes his moan,
Walks early out, and ever is alone.
Nor, mixed in mirth, in youthful pleasure shares,
But sighs when songs and instruments he hears.
His spirits are so low, his voice is drowned,
He hears as from afar, or in a swound,
Like the deaf murmurs of a distant sound:
Uncombed his locks, and squalid his attire,
Unlike the trim of love and gay desire;
But full of museful mopings, which presage
The loss of reason, and conclude in rage.[1]

This when he had endured a year and more,
Now wholly changed from what he was before,
It happened once, that slumbering as he lay,
He dreamt (his dream began at break of day)
That Hermes o'er his head in air appeared,
And with soft words his drooping spirits cheered:
His hat, adorned with wings, disclosed the god,

[1] Insanity.

And in his hand he bore the sleep-compelling rod:
Such as he seemed, when at his sire's command
On Argus' head he laid the snaky wand.
"Arise!" he said, "to conquering Athens go;
There fate appoints an end to all thy woe!"
The fright awakened Arcite with a start,
Against his bosom bounced his heaving heart;
But soon he said, with scarce-recovered breath,
"And thither will I go, to meet my death,
Sure to be slain; but death is my desire,
Since in Emilia's sight I shall expire!"
By chance he spied a mirror while he spoke,
And gazing there, beheld his altered look:
Wondering, he saw his features and his hue
So much were changed, that scarce himself he knew.
A sudden thought then starting in his mind:
"Since I in Arcite cannot Arcite find,
The world may search in vain with all their eyes,
But never penetrate through this disguise.
Thanks to the change which grief and sickness give,
In low estate I may securely live,
And see, unknown, my mistress day by day."
He said; and clothed himself in coarse array,
A laboring hind in show; then forth he went,
And to the Athenian towers his journey bent·
One squire attended in the same disguise,
Made conscious of his master's enterprise.
Arrived at Athens, soon he came to Court,
Unknown, unquestioned, in that thick resort;
Proffering for hire his service at the gate,
To drudge, draw water, and to run or wait.

So fair befell him, that for little gain
He served at first Emilia's chamberlain;
And, watchful all advantages to spy,
Was still at hand, and in his master's eye;
And as his bones were big, and sinews strong,
Refused no toil that could to slaves belong:
But from deep wells with engines water drew,
And used his noble hands the wood to hew.
He passed a year at least attending thus
On Emily, and called Philostratus.
But never was there man of his degree
So much esteemed, so well beloved as he.
So gentle of condition was he known,
That through the Court his courtesy was blown:
All think him worthy of a greater place,
And recommend him to the royal grace;
That, exercised within a higher sphere,
His virtues more conspicuous might appear.
Thus by the general voice was Arcite praised,
And by great Theseus to high favor raised;
Among his menial servants first enrolled,
And largely entertained[1] with sums of gold:
Besides what secretly from Thebes was sent,
Of his own income, and his annual rent;
This well employed, he purchased friends and fame,
But cautiously concealed from whence it came.
Thus for three years he lived with large increase,
In arms, of honor; and esteem, in peace;
To Theseus' person he was ever near,
And Theseus for his virtues held him dear.

[1] Generously maintained and paid.

While Arcite lives in bliss, the story turns
Where hopeless Palamon in prison mourns.
For six long years immured, the captive knight
Had dragged his chains, and scarcely seen the light:
Lost liberty and love at once he bore;
His prison pained him much, his passion more:
Nor dares he hope his fetters to remove,
Nor ever wishes to be free from love.
But when the sixth revolving year was run,
And May within the Twins received the sun;[1]
Were it by chance, or forceful destiny,
Which forms in causes first whate'er shall be,
Assisted by a friend, one moonless night,
This Palamon from prison took his flight:
A pleasant beverage he prepared before,
Of wine and honey mixed, with added store
Of opium; to his keeper this he brought,
Who swallowed unaware the sleepy draught,
And snored secure till morn, his senses bound
In slumber, and in long oblivion drowned.
Short was the night, and careful Palamon
Sought the next covert ere the rising sun.
A thick-spread forest near the city lay,
To this with lengthened strides he took his way,
(For far he could not fly, and feared the day.)
Safe from pursuit, he meant to shun the light,
Till the brown shadows of the friendly night
To Thebes might favor his intended flight.
When to his country come, his next design
Was all the Theban race in arms to join,
And war on Theseus, till he lost his life,
Or won the beauteous Emily to wife.

[1] When the sun enters that sign of the zodiac known as the Gemini, or Twins.

Thus while his thoughts the lingering day beguile,
To gentle Arcite let us turn our style;
Who little dreamt how nigh he was to care,
Till treacherous fortune caught him in the snare.
The morning lark, the messenger of day,
Saluted in her song the morning gray;
And soon the sun arose with beams so bright
That all the horizon laughed to see the joyous
sight:
He with his tepid rays the rose renews,
And licks the drooping leaves, and dries the dews,
When Arcite left his bed, resolved to pay
Observance to the month of merry May;
Forth on his fiery steed betimes he rode,
That scarcely prints the turf on which he trod:
At ease he seemed, and prancing o'er the plains,
Turned only to the grove his horse's reins,
The grove I named before; and, lighted there,
A woodbine garland sought to crown his hair;
Then turned his face against the rising day,
And raised his voice to welcome in the May:—
"For thee, sweet month, the groves green liveries
wear,
If not the first, the fairest of the year:
For thee the Graces lead the dancing Hours,
And Nature's ready pencil paints the flowers:
When thy short reign is past, the feverish sun
The sultry tropic fears, and moves more slowly on.
So may thy tender blossoms fear no blight,
Nor goats, with venomed teeth, thy tendrils bite,
As thou shalt guide my wandering feet to find
The fragrant greens I seek, my brows to bind."

His vows addressed, within the grove he strayed,
Till fate, or fortune, near the place conveyed
His steps where secret Palamon was laid.
Full little thought of him the gentle knight,
Who, flying death, had there concealed his flight,
In brakes and brambles hid, and shunning mortal
sight;
And less he knew him for his hated foe,
But feared him as a man he did not know.
But as it has been said of ancient years,
That fields are full of eyes, and woods have ears;
For this the wise are ever on their guard,
For unforeseen (they say) is unprepared.
Uncautious Arcite thought himself alone,
And less than all suspected Palamon;
Who, listening, heard him, while he searched the grove,
And loudly sung his roundelay of love.
But on the sudden stopped, and silent stood,
(As lovers often muse and change their mood;
Now high as heaven, and then as low as hell;
Now up, now down, as buckets in a well:
For Venus, like her day, will change her cheer,
And seldom shall we see a Friday clear.)
Thus Arcite having sung, with altered hue
Sunk on the ground, and from his bosom drew
A desperate sigh, accusing heaven and fate,
And angry Juno's unrelenting hate:—
"Cursed be the day when first I did appear;
Let it be blotted from the calendar,
Lest it pollute the month, and poison all the year.
Still will the jealous queen pursue our race?
Cadmus is dead, the Theban city was:

Yet ceases not her hate: for all who come
From Cadmus are involved in Cadmus' doom.
I suffer for my blood: unjust decree!
That punishes another's crime on me.
In mean estate I serve my mortal foe,
The man who caused my country's overthrow.
This is not all; for Juno, to my shame,
Has forced me to forsake my former name!
Arcite I was, Philostratus I am.
That side of heaven is all my enemy:
Mars ruined Thebes: his mother ruined me.
Of all the royal race remains but one
Beside myself, the unhappy Palamon,
Whom Theseus holds in bonds and will not free;
Without a crime, except his kin to me.
Yet these, and all the rest, I could endure;
But love's a malady without a cure:
Fierce love has pierced me with his fiery dart,
He fires within, and hisses at my heart.
Your eyes, fair Emily, my fate pursue;
I suffer for the rest, I die for you.
Of such a goddess no time leaves record,
Who burned the temple where she was adored:
And let it burn, I never will complain,
Pleased with my sufferings, if you knew my pain.''

At this a sickly qualm his heart assailed,
His ears ring inward, and his senses failed.
No word missed Palamon of all he spoke,
But soon to deadly pale he changed his look:
He trembled every limb, and felt a smart,
As if cold steel had glided through his heart;

Nor longer staid, but starting from his place,
Discovered stood, and showed his hostile face:
"False traitor Arcite! traitor to thy blood!
Bound by thy sacred oath to seek my good,
Now art thou found forsworn, for Emily;
And dar'st attempt her love, for whom I die.
So hast thou cheated Theseus with a wile,
Against thy vow, returning to beguile
Under a borrowed name: as false to me,
So false thou art to him who set thee free:
But rest assured, that either thou shalt die,
Or else renounce thy claim in Emily:
For though unarmed I am and (freed by chance)
Am here without my sword, or pointed lance:
Hope not, base man, unquestioned hence to go,
For I am Palamon, thy mortal foe."

Arcite, who heard this tale, and knew the man,
His sword unsheathed, and fiercely thus began:
"Now, by the gods who govern Heaven above,
Wert thou not weak with hunger, mad with love,
That word had been thy last; or in this grove
This hand should force thee to renounce thy love.
The surety which I gave thee, I defy;
Fool, not to know that love endures no tie;
And Jove but laughs at lover's perjury.
Know I will serve thee fair in thy despite;
But since thou art my kinsman, and a knight,
Here, have my faith: to-morrow in this grove
Our arms shall plead the titles of our love:
And Heaven so help my right, as I alone

Will come, and keep the cause and quarrel both
unknown;
With arms of proof both for myself and thee;
Choose thou the best, and leave the worst to me.
And that at better ease thou may'st abide,
Bedding and clothes I will this night provide,
And needful sustenance, that thou may'st be
A conquest better won, and worthy me."
His promise Palamon accepts; but prayed
To keep it better than the first he made.
Thus fair they parted till the morrow's dawn;
For each had laid his plighted faith to pawn.

Oh, Love! thou sternly dost thy power maintain,
And wilt not bear a rival in thy reign;
Tyrants and thou all fellowship disdain.
This was in Arcite proved and Palamon,
Both in despair, yet each would love alone.
Arcite returned and, as in honor tied,
His foe with bedding and with food supplied;
Then ere the day two suits of armor sought,
Which borne before him on his steed he brought;
Both were of shining steel, and wrought so pure,
As might the strokes of two such arms endure.
Now, at the time, and in the appointed place,
The challenger and challenged, face to face,
Approach; each other from afar they knew,
And from afar their hatred changed their hue.
So stands the Thracian herdsman with his spear,
Full in the gap, and hopes the hunted bear,
And hears him rustling in the wood, and sees
His course at distance by the bending trees;

And thinks, "Here comes my mortal enemy,
And either he must fall in fight, or I":
This while he thinks, he lifts aloft his dart;
A generous chillness seizes every part;
The veins pour back the blood, and fortify the heart.

Thus pale they meet; their eyes with fury burn;
None greets; for none the greeting will return:
But in dumb surliness, each armed with care
His foe professed, as brother of the war:
Then both, no moment lost, at once advance
Against each other, armed with sword and lance:
They lash, they foin, they pass, they strive to bore
Their corslets and the thinnest parts explore.
Thus two long hours in equal arms they stood,
And wounded, wound; till both were bathed in blood;
And not a foot of ground had either got,
As if the world depended on the spot.
Fell Arcite like an angry tiger fared,
And like a lion Palamon appeared;
Or as two boars whom love to battle draws,
With rising bristles, and with frothy jaws,
Their adverse breasts with tusks oblique they wound,
With grunts and groans the forest rings around:
So fought the knights, and fighting must abide,
Till fate an umpire send their difference to decide.

The power that ministers to God's decrees,
And executes on earth what Heaven foresees,
Called Providence, or Chance, or fatal sway,
Comes with resistless force, and finds or makes her way.
Nor kings, nor nations, nor united power,

One moment can retard the appointed hour;
And some one day, some wondrous chance appears,
Which happened not in centuries of years:
For sure, whate'er we mortals hate or love,
Or hope or fear, depends on Powers above;
They move our appetites to good or ill,
And by foresight necessitate the will.
In Theseus this appears; whose youthful joy
Was beasts of chase in forests to destroy:
This gentle knight, inspired by jolly May,
Forsook his easy couch at early day,
And to the woods and wilds pursued his way.
Beside him rode Hippolita, the queen,
And Emily attired in lively green.
With horns, and hounds, and all the tuneful cry,
To hunt a royal hart within the covert nigh:
And as he followed Mars before, so now
He serves the goddess of the silver bow.[1]
The way that Theseus took was to the wood
Where the two knights in cruel battle stood:
The land on which they fought, the appointed place
In which the uncoupled hounds began the chase.
Thither forthright he rode to rouse the prey,
That shaded by the fern in harbor lay;
And thence dislodged, was wont to leave the wood
For open fields, and cross the crystal flood.
Approached, and looking underneath the sun,
He saw proud Arcite and fierce Palamon
In mortal battle, doubling blow on blow;
Like lightning flamed their falchions to and fro,
And shot a dreadful gleam; so strong they struck,
There seemed less force required to fell an oak.

[1] Diana, the Huntress.

He gazed with wonder on their equal might,
Looked eager on, but knew not either knight;
Resolved to learn, he spurred his fiery steed
With goring rowels, to provoke his speed.
The minute ended that began the race,
So soon he was betwixt them on the place;
And with his sword unsheathed, on pain of life
Commands both combatants to cease their strife:
Then with imperious tone pursues his threat:
"What are you? Why in arms together met?
How dares your pride presume against my laws,
As in a listed field to fight your cause,
Unasked the royal grant; no marshal by,
As knightly rites require; no judge to try?"
Then Palamon, with scarce recovered breath,
Thus hasty spoke: "We both deserve the death,
And both would die; for look the world around,
A pair so wretched is not to be found.
Our life's a load; encumbered with the charge,
We long to set the imprisoned soul at large.
Now as thou art a sovereign judge, decree
The rightful doom of death to him and me;
Let neither find thy grace; for grace is cruelty.
Me first! O kill me first! and cure my woe;
Then sheathe the sword of justice on my foe:
Or kill him first; for when his name is heard,
He, foremost, will receive his due reward.
Arcite of Thebes is he, thy mortal foe,
On whom thy grace did liberty bestow;
But first contracted, that if ever found
By day or night upon the Athenian ground,
His head should pay the forfeit: see returned

The perjured knight, his oath and honor scorned!
For this is he, who, with a borrowed name,
And proffered service, to thy palace came,
Now called Philostratus: retained by thee,
A traitor trusted, and in high degree,
Aspiring to the hand of beauteous Emily.
My part remains:—From Thebes my birth I own,
And call myself the unhappy Palamon.
Think me not like that man; since no disgrace
Can force me to renounce the honor of my race;
Know me for what I am; I broke thy chain,
Nor promised I thy prisoner to remain:
The love of liberty with life is given,
And life itself the inferior gift of Heaven.
Thus without crime I fled; but further know,
I, with this Arcite, am thy mortal foe:
Then give me death, since I thy life pursue,
For safeguard of thyself, death is my due.
More wouldst thou know? I love bright Emily,
And for her sake and in her sight will die:
But kill my rival too; for he no less
Deserves; and I thy righteous doom will bless;
Assured that what I lose, he never shall possess."
To this replied the stern Athenian prince,
And sourly smiled, "In owning your offense
You judge yourself; and I but keep record
In place of law, while you pronounce the word.
Take your desert, the death you have decreed;
I seal your doom, and ratify the deed.
By Mars, the patron of my arms, you die!"

He said: dumb sorrow seized the standers-by.
The queen above the rest, by nature good,
(The pattern formed of perfect womanhood)
For tender pity wept: when she began,
Through the bright choir the infectious virtue ran.
All dropped their tears, e'en the contended maid;
And thus among themselves they softly said:
"What eyes can suffer this unworthy sight!
Two youths of royal blood, renowned in fight,
The mastership of Heaven in face and mind,
And lovers, far beyond their faithless kind:
See their wide streaming wounds; they neither came
For pride of empire, nor desire of fame:
Kings fight for kingdoms, madmen for applause;
But love for love alone; that crowns the lover's cause!"
This thought, which ever bribes the beauteous kind,
Such pity wrought in every lady's mind,
They left their steeds, and prostrate on the place,
From the fierce king implored the offenders' grace.

He paused awhile, stood silent in his mood
(For yet his rage was boiling in his blood),
But soon his tender mind the impression felt
(As softest metals are not slow to melt,
And pity soonest runs in softest minds),
Then reasons with himself; and first he finds
His passion cast a mist before his sense,
And either made, or magnified the offense.
Offense! of what? to whom? Who judged the cause?
The prisoner freed himself by nature's laws:
Born free, he sought his right: the man he freed
Was perjured, but his love excused the deed.

Thus pondering, he looked under with his eyes,
And saw the women's tears, and heard their cries;
Which moved compassion more; he shook his head,
And softly sighing to himself he said:—
"Curse on the unpardoning prince, whom tears can draw
To no remorse; who rules by lions' law;
And deaf to prayers, by no submission bowed,
Rends all alike, the penitent and proud."
At this, with look serene, he raised his head,
Reason resumed her place, and passion fled;
Then thus aloud he spoke: "The power of love,
In earth, and seas, and air, and heaven above,
Rules, unresisted, with an awful nod;
By daily miracles declared a god:
He blinds the wise, gives eyesight to the blind;
And moulds and stamps anew the lover's mind.
Behold that Arcite, and this Palamon,
Freed from my fetters, and in safety gone;
What hindered either in their native soil
At ease to reap the harvest of their toil?
But Love, their lord, did otherwise ordain,
And brought them in their own despite again,
To suffer death deserved; for well they know,
'Tis in my power, and I their deadly foe;
The proverb holds, that to be wise and love,
Is hardly granted to the gods above.
See how the madmen bleed: behold the gains
With which their master, Love, rewards their pains.
For seven long years, on duty every day,
Lo! their obedience, and their monarch's pay:
Yet, as in duty bound, they serve him on;

And ask the fools, they think it wisely done:
Nor ease, nor wealth, nor life itself regard,
For 'tis their maxim, love is love's reward.
This is not all; the fair, for whom they strove,
Nor knew before, nor could suspect their love,
Nor thought, when she beheld the sight from far,
Her beauty was the occasion of the war.
But sure a general doom on man is passed,
And all are fools and lovers, first or last:
This both by others and myself I know,
For I have served their sovereign long ago;
Oft have been caught within the winding train
Of female snares, and felt the lover's pain,
And learned how far the god can human hearts constrain.
To this remembrance, and the prayers of those
Who for the offending warriors interpose,
I give their forfeit lives; on this accord,[1]
To do me homage as their sovereign lord;
And as my vassals, to their utmost might
Assist my person, and assert my right."

This freely sworn, the knights their grace obtained;
Then thus the king his secret thoughts explained:
"If wealth, or honor, or a royal race,
Or each, or all, may win a lady's grace,
Then either of you knights may well deserve
A princess born; and such is she you serve:
For Emily is sister to the crown,
And but too well to both her beauty known:
As therefore both are equal in degree,
The lot of both be left to destiny.

[1] Agreement.

Now hear the award, and happy may it prove
To her, and him who best deserves her love.
Depart from thence in peace and, free as air,
Search the wide world, and where you please repair;
But on the day when this returning sun
To the same point through every sign has run,
Then each of you his hundred knights shall bring,
In royal lists to fight before the king;
And then the knight whom fate or happy chance
Shall with his friends to victory advance,
And grace his arms so far in equal fight,
From out the bars to force his opposite,
Or kill, or make him recreant on the plain,
The prize of valor and of love shall gain;
The vanquished party shall their claim release,
And the long jars conclude in lasting peace.
The charge be mine to adorn the chosen ground,
The theater of war, for champions so renowned;
And take the patron's place, of either knight,
With eyes impartial to behold the fight;
And Heaven of me so judge as I shall judge aright.
If both are satisfied with this accord,
Swear by the laws of knighthood on my sword."

Who now but Palamon exults with joy?
And ravished Arcite seems to touch the sky.
The whole assembled troop was pleased as well,
Extolled the award, and on their knees they fell
To bless the gracious king. The knights with leave
Departing from the place, his last commands receive;
On Emily with equal ardor look,
And from her eyes their inspiration took;

From thence to Thebes' old walls pursue their way,
Each to provide his champions for the day.

PART III

It might be deemed, on our historian's part,
Or too much negligence, or want of art,
If he forgot the vast magnificence
Of royal Theseus, and his large expense.
He first enclosed for lists a level ground,
The whole circumference a mile around:
The form was circular; and all without
A trench was sunk, to moat the place about.
Within an amphitheater appeared,
Raised in degrees;[1] to sixty paces reared;
That when a man was placed in one degree,
Height was allowed for him above to see.
Eastward was built a gate of marble white;
The like adorned the western opposite.
A nobler object than his fabric was
Rome never saw; nor of so vast a space.
For rich with spoils of many a conquered land,
All arts and artists Theseus could command;
Who sold for hire, or wrought for better fame,
The master painters and the carvers came.
So rose within the compass of the year
An age's work, a glorious theater.
Then o'er its eastern gate was raised above
A temple, sacred to the Queen of Love;
An altar stood below: on either hand
A priest with roses crowned, who held a myrtle wand.

[1] Steps.

The dome of Mars was on the gate opposed,
And on the north a turret was enclosed,
Within the wall, of alabaster white
And crimson coral, for the Queen of Night;[1]
Who takes in sylvan sports her chaste delight.

Within these oratories might you see
Rich carvings, portraitures, and imagery:
Where every figure to the life expressed
The godhead's power to whom it was addressed.
In Venus' temple on the sides were seen
The broken slumbers of enamored men;
Prayers that e'en spoke, and pity seemed to call,
And issuing sighs that smoked along the wall,
Beauty, and youth, and wealth, and luxury,
And sprightly hope, and short-enduring joy;
Expense, and after-thought, and idle care,
And doubts of motley hue, and dark despair;
Suspicions, and fantastical surmise,
And Jealousy suffused,[2] with jaundice in her eyes,
Discoloring all she viewed, in tawny dressed,
Down looked, and with a cuckoo on her fist.
Opposed to her, on the other side, advance
The costly feast, the carol, and the dance,
Minstrels and music, poetry and play,
And balls by night, and tournaments by day.
All these were painted on the wall, and more;
With acts and monuments of times before:
And others added by prophetic doom,
And lovers yet unborn, and loves to come:
For there the Idalian Mount, and Citheron,
The Court of Venus, was in colors drawn:

[1] Cynthia or Phoebe, goddess of the moon, is Diana on earth.
[2] With skin yellow, as in jaundice.

Before the palace gate, in careless dress,
In loose array, sat portress Idleness:
There, by the fount, Narcissus pined alone;
There Samson was, with wiser Solomon,
And all the mighty names by love undone:
Medea's charms were there, Circean feasts,
With bowls that turned enamored youths to beasts.
Here might be seen that beauty, wealth, and wit,
And prowess to the power of Love submit:
The spreading snare for all mankind is laid;
And lovers all betray, and are betrayed.
The goddess' self some noble hand had wrought;
Smiling she seemed, and full of pleasing thought:
From ocean as she first began to rise,
And smoothed the ruffled seas, and cleared the skies;
A lute she held; and on her head was seen
A wreath of roses red, and myrtles green:
Her turtles fanned the buxom air above;
And by his mother stood an infant Love
With wings unfledged; his eyes were banded o'er;
His hands a bow, his back a quiver bore,
Supplied with arrows bright and keen, a deadly store.

But in the dome of mighty Mars the red
With different figures all the sides were spread;
This temple, less in form, with equal grace
Was imitative of the first in Thrace:
For that cold region was the loved abode
And sovereign mansion of the warrior-god.
The landscape was a forest wide and bare,
Where neither beast nor human kind repair:
The fowl, that scent afar, the borders fly,

And shun the bitter blast, and wheel about the sky.
A cake of scurf lies baking on the ground,
And prickly stubs, instead of trees, are found;
Or woods with knots and knares deformed and old;
Headless the most, and hideous to behold:
A rattling tempest through the branches went,
That stripped them bare, and one sole way they bent.
Heaven froze above, severe; the clouds congeal,
And through the crystal vault appeared the standing hail.
Such was the face without; a mountain stood
Threatening from high, and overlooked the wood;
Beneath the lowering brow, and on a bent,
The temple stood of Mars armipotent:
The frame of burnished steel, that cast a glare
From far, and seemed to thaw the freezing air.
A straight long entry to the temple led,
Blind with high walls, and horror overhead:
Thence issued such a blast, and hollow roar,
As threatened from the hinge to heave the door;
In through that door a northern light there shone;
'Twas all it had, for windows there were none.
The gate was adamant; eternal frame!
Which, hewed by Mars himself, from Indian quarries came,
The labor of a god; and all along
Tough iron plates were clenched to make it strong.
A ton about was every pillar there;
A polished mirror shone not half so clear.
There saw I how the secret felon wrought,
And treason laboring in the traitor's thought.
There the red Anger dared the pallid Fear;

Next stood Hypocrisy, with holy leer
Soft-smiling, and demurely looking down,
But hid the dagger underneath the gown:
The assassinating wife, the household fiend;
And far the blackest there, the traitor-friend.
On the other side there stood Destruction bare;
Unpunished rapine, and a waste of war.
Contest, with sharpened knives, in cloisters drawn,
And all with blood bespread the holy lawn.
Loud menaces were heard, and foul Disgrace,
And bawling Infamy, in language base;
Till Sense was lost in sound, and Silence fled the place.
The slayer of himself yet saw I there,
The gore congealed was clotted in his hair;
With eyes half closed, and gaping mouth he lay,
And grim, as when he breathed his sullen soul away.
In midst of all the dome Misfortune sate,
And gloomy Discontent, and fell Debate;
And Madness laughing in his ireful mood;
And armed Complaint on theft—and cries of blood.
There was a murdered corpse, in covert laid,
And violent death in thousand shapes displayed:
The city to the soldier's rage resigned:
Successful wars, and poverty behind:
Ships burnt in fight, or forced on rocky shores,
And the rash hunter strangled by the boars:
The new-born babe by nurses overlaid;
And the cook caught within the raging fire he made.
All ills of Mars's nature, flame and steel;
The gasping charioteer beneath the wheel
Of his own car; the ruined house that falls
And intercepts her lord betwixt the walls:

The whole division that to Mars pertains,
All trades of death that deal in steel for gains,
Were there: the butcher, armorer, and smith
Who forges sharpened falchions, or the scythe.
The scarlet Conquest on a tower was placed,
With shouts and soldiers' acclamations graced:
A pointed sword hung threatening o'er his head,
Sustained but by a slender twine of thread.

Canterbury Cathedral, Tomb of the Black Prince

There saw I Mars's Ides,[1] the Capitol,
The seer in vain foretelling Caesar's fall,
The last triumvirs, and the wars they move,
And Anthony, who lost the world for love.
These, and a thousand more, the fane adorn;
Their fates were painted ere the men were born;
All copied from the heavens, and ruling force
Of the red star, in his revolving course.
The form of Mars high on a chariot stood,
All sheathed in arms, and gruffly looked the god.

[1] On the Ides (the fifteenth) of March, Caesar was slain in Rome, though not actually in the Capitol.

Tired with deformities of death, I haste
To the third temple of Diana chaste:—
A sylvan scene with various greens was drawn,
Shades on the sides, and on the midst a lawn:
The silver Cynthia, with her nymphs around,
Pursued the flying deer, the woods with horns resound:
Calisto there stood manifest of shame,
And, turned a bear, the northern star became:
Her son was next, and by peculiar grace
In the cold circle held the second place:
The stag Actaeon in the stream had spied
The naked huntress, and, for seeing, died:
His hounds, unknowing of his change, pursue
The chase, and their mistaken master slew.
Peneian Daphne too was there to see,
Apollo's love before, and now his tree;
The adjoining fane the assembled Greeks expressed,
And hunting of the Calydonian beast;
Œnides' valor, and his envied prize;
The fatal power of Atalanta's eyes;
Diana's vengeance on the victor shown,
The murdress mother, and consuming son;
The Volscian queen extended on the plain;
The treason punished, and the traitor slain.
The rest were various huntings, well designed,
And savage beasts destroyed, of every kind.
The graceful goddess was arrayed in green;
About her feet were little beagles[1] seen,
That watched with upward eyes the motions of their
queen.
Her legs were buskined, and the left before,
In act to shoot; a silver bow she bore,

[1] Hounds.

And at her back a painted quiver wore.
She trod a waxing moon, that soon would wane
And, drinking borrowed light, be filled again:
With downcast eyes, as seeming to survey
The dark dominions, her alternate sway.
All these the painter drew with such command,
That Nature snatched the pencil from his hand;
Theseus beheld the fanes of every god,
And thought his mighty cost was well bestowed.

The theater thus raised, the lists enclosed,
And all with vast magnificence disposed,
We leave the monarch pleased; and haste to bring
The knights to combat; and their arms to sing.

PART IV

The day approached when fortune should decide
The important enterprise, and give the bride;
For now, the rivals round the world had sought,
And each his number, well appointed, brought.
The nations far and near contend in choice,
And send the flower of war by public voice;
That after, or before, were never known
Such chiefs; as each an army seem'd alone.
Beside the champions, all of high degree,
Who knighthood loved, and deeds of chivalry,
Thronged to the lists, and envied to behold
The names of others, not their own, enrolled.
Nor seems it strange; for every noble knight
Who loves the fair, and is endued with might,
In such a quarrel would be proud to fight.
There breathes not scarce a man on British ground

(An isle for love and arms of old renowned)
But would have sold his life to purchase fame.
A hundred knights with Palamon there came,
Approved in fight, and men of mighty name;
Their arms were several, as their nations were,
But furnished all alike with sword and spear.
Some wore coat-armor, imitating scale;
And next their skins were stubborn shirts of mail.
Some wore a breastplate and a light jupon,[1]
Their horses clothed with rich caparison:
Some for defense would leathern bucklers use
Of folded hides; and others, shields of Pruce.[2]
One hung a poleaxe at his saddle-bow,
And one a heavy mace, to stun the foe:
One for his legs and knees provided well,
With jambeaux[3] armed, and double plates of steel:
This on his helmet wore a lady's glove,
And that, a sleeve embroidered by his love.

With Palamon, above the rest in place,
Lycurgus came, the surly King of Thrace;
Black was his beard, and manly was his face;
The balls of his broad eyes rolled in his head,
And glared betwixt a yellow and a red:
He looked a lion with a gloomy stare,
And o'er his eyebrows hung his matted hair:
Big-boned, and large of limbs, with sinews strong,
Broad-shouldered, and his arms were round and long.
Four milk-white bulls (the Thracian use[4] of old)
Were yoked to draw his car of burnished gold.
Upright he stood, and bore aloft his shield,
Conspicuous from afar, and overlooked the field.

[1] A close coat.
[2] Prussian leather.
[3] Leg-armor.
[4] Custom.

His surcoat was a bear-skin on his back;
His hair hung long behind, and glossy raven-black.
His ample forehead bore a coronet,
With sparkling diamonds and with rubies set:
Ten brace, and more, of greyhounds, snowy fair,
And tall as stags, ran loose, and coursed around his chair;
A match for pards[1] in flight, in grappling for the bear:
With golden muzzles all their mouths were bound,
And collars of the same their necks surround.
Thus through the fields Lycurgus took his way:
His hundred knights attend in pomp and proud array.

To match this monarch, with strong Arcite came
Emetrius, King of Ind, a mighty name;
On a bay courser, goodly to behold,
The trappings of his horse embossed with barbarous gold.
Not Mars bestrode a steed with greater grace;
His surcoat o'er his arms was cloth of Thrace,
Adorned with pearls, all orient, round, and great;
His saddle was of gold, with emeralds set.
His shoulders large a mantle did attire,
With rubies thick, and sparkling as the fire:
His amber-colored locks in ringlets run
With graceful negligence, and shone against the sun.
His nose was aquiline, his eyes were blue,
Ruddy his lips, and fresh and fair his hue:
Some sprinkled freckles on his face were seen,
Whose dusk set off the whiteness of the skin.
His awful presence did the crowd surprise,
Nor durst the rash spectator meet his eyes;

[1] Leopards.

Eyes that confessed him born for kingly sway,
So fierce, they flashed intolerable day.
His age in nature's youthful prime appeared,
And just began to bloom his yellow beard;
Whene'er he spoke, his voice was heard around,
Loud as a trumpet, with a silver sound;
A laurel wreathed his temples, fresh and green,
And myrtle sprigs, the marks of love, were mixed
 between;
Upon his fist he bore, for his delight,
An eagle well reclaimed[1] and lily-white.

His hundred knights attend him to the war,
All armed for battle, save their heads were bare.
Words and devices blazed on every shield,
And pleasing was the terror of the field.
For kings, and dukes, and barons you might see,
Like sparkling stars, though different in degree,
All for the increase of arms, and love of chivalry.
Before the king tame leopards led the way,
And troops of lions innocently play.

In this array the war of either side
Through Athens passed with military pride.
At prime[2] they entered on the Sunday morn;
Rich tapestry spread the streets, and flowers the posts
 adorn.
The town was all a jubilee of feasts;
So Theseus willed, in honor of his guests.
Himself with open arms the kings embraced;
Then all the rest in their degrees were graced.
No harbinger[3] was needful for the night,
For every house was proud to lodge a knight.

---

1 Tamed and disciplined.
2 About nine o'clock.
3 Messenger to engage lodging.

I pass the royal treat, nor must relate
The gifts bestowed, nor how the champions sate;
Who first, who last, or how the knights addressed
Their vows, or who was fairest at the feast;
Whose voice, whose graceful dance, did most surprise;
Soft amorous sighs, and silent love of eyes.
The rivals call my Muse another way,
To sing their vigils for the ensuing day.

'Twas ebbing darkness, past the noon of night,
And Phosphor, on the confines of the light,
Promised the sun, ere day began to spring;
The tuneful lark already stretched her wing,
And flickering on her nest made short essays to sing;
When wakeful Palamon, preventing[1] day,
Took to the royal lists his early way,
To Venus at her fane, in her own house, to pray.
There falling on his knees before her shrine,
He thus implored with prayers her power divine:—
"Creator Venus! genial Power of Love!
The bliss of men below and gods above!
Thou gladder of the mount of Cytheron,
Increase[2] of Jove, companion of the sun!
If e'er Adonis touched thy tender heart,
Have pity, goddess, for thou know'st the smart.
Alas! I have not words to tell my grief;
To vent my sorrow would be some relief:
Light sufferings give us leisure to complain;
We groan, but cannot speak, in greater pain.
O goddess! tell thyself what I would say;
Thou know'st it, and I feel too much to pray.
So grant my suit as I enforce my might,

[1] Anticipating.
[2] Child.

In love to be thy champion and thy knight;
A servant to thy sex, a slave to thee,
A foe professed to barren chastity.
Nor ask I fame or honor of the field;
Nor choose I more to vanquish than to yield:
In my divine Emilia make me blest,
Let Fate or partial Chance dispose the rest:
Find thou the manner and the means prepare;
Possession, more than conquest, is my care.
Mars is the warrior's god; in him it lies,
On whom he favors to confer the prize;
With smiling aspect you serenely move
In your fifth orb, and rule the realm of love.
But if you this ambitious prayer deny,
(A wish, I grant, beyond mortality)
Then let me sink beneath proud Arcite's arms,
And I once dead, let him possess her charms."

Thus ended he: then with observance due
The sacred incense on her altar threw.
The curling smoke mounts heavy from the fires;
At length it catches flame, and in a blaze expires;
At once the gracious goddess gave the sign,
Her statue shook, and trembled all the shrine.
Pleased, Palamon the tardy omen took;
For, since the flames pursued the trailing smoke,
He knew his boon was granted; but the day
To distance driven, and joy adjourned with long delay.

Now morn with rosy light had streaked the sky,
Up rose the sun, and up rose Emily;
Addressed her early steps to Cynthia's fane,

In state, attended by her maiden train,
Who bore the vests that holy rites require,
Incense, and odorous gums, and covered fire.
The plenteous horns with pleasant mead they crown,
Nor wanted aught besides in honor of the Moon.
Now while the temple smoked with hallowed steam,
They wash the virgin in a living stream.
The secret ceremonies I conceal,
Uncouth, perhaps unlawful, to reveal:
But such they were as pagan use required,
Performed by women when the men retired.
Well-meaners think no harm; but for the rest,
Things sacred they pervert, and silence is the best.
Her shining hair, uncombed, was loosely spread,
A crown of mastless oak adorned her head,
When, to the shrine approached, the spotless maid
Had kindling fires on either altar laid
(The rites were such as were observed of old,
By Statius in his Theban story told);
Then kneeling, with her hands across her breast,
Thus lowly she preferred her chaste request:—

"O goddess! haunter of the woodland green,
To whom both heaven, and earth, and seas are seen;
Queen of the nether skies, where half the year
Thy silver beams descend, and light the gloomy sphere;
Goddess of maids! and conscious of our hearts,
So keep me from the vengeance of thy darts,
Which Niobe's devoted issue felt,
When hissing through the skies the feathered deaths were dealt;
As I desire to live a virgin life,

Nor know the name of mother or of wife.
Thy votaress from my tender years I am,
And love, like thee, the woods and sylvan game.
Like death, thou know'st, I loath the nuptial state;
And man, the tyrant of our sex, I hate;
A lowly servant, but a lofty mate.
Now by thy triple shape, as thou art seen
In heaven,[1] earth,[2] hell,[3] and everywhere a queen,
Grant this my first desire: let discord cease,
And make betwixt the rivals lasting peace;
Quench their hot fire, or far from me remove
The flame, and turn it on some other love.
Or if my frowning stars have so decreed
That one must be rejected, one succeed,
Make him my lord, within whose faithful breast
Is fixed my image, and who loves me best.
But, oh! even that avert! I choose it not;
But take it as the least unhappy lot.
A maid I am, and of thy virgin train;
Oh, let me still that spotless name retain!
Frequent the forests, thy chaste will obey,
And only make the beasts of chase my prey!"

The flames ascend on either altar clear,
While thus the blameless maid addressed her prayer.
When lo! the burning fire that shone so bright,
Flew off, all sudden, with extinguished light,
And left one altar dark, a little space,
Which turned, self-kindled, and renewed the blaze:
The other victor-flame a moment stood,
Then fell, and lifeless left the extinguished wood;
Forever lost, the irrevocable light

1 Cynthia, or Phoebe.
2 Diana.
3 Hecate.

Forsook the blackening coals and sunk to night:
At either end it whistled as it flew.
And as the brands were green, so dropped the dew,
Infected, as it fell, with sweat of sanguine hue.

The maid from that ill omen turned her eyes,
And with loud shrieks and clamors rent the skies;
Nor knew what signified the boding sign,
But found the Powers displeased, and feared the wrath divine.
Then shook the sacred shrine, and sudden light
Sprung through the vaulted roof, and made the temple bright.
The Power, behold! the Power in glory shone,
By her bent bow and her keen arrows known;
The rest, a huntress issuing from the wood,
Reclining on her cornel spear she stood;
Then gracious thus began:—"Dismiss thy fear,
And Heaven's unchanged decrees attentive hear:
More powerful gods have torn thee from my side,
Unwilling to resign, and doomed a bride:
The two contending knights are weighed above;
One Mars protects, and one the Queen of Love;
But which the man, is in the Thunderer's breast,
This he pronounced—' 'Tis he who loves thee best.'
The fire that, once extinct, revived again,
Foreshows the love allotted to remain:
Farewell!" she said; and vanished from the place:
The sheaf of arrows shook, and rattled in the case.
Aghast at this, the royal virgin stood
Disclaimed, and now no more a sister of the wood:
But to the parting goddess thus she prayed:

"Propitious still be present to my aid,
Nor quite abandon your once-favored maid!"
Then, sighing, she returned; but smiled betwixt,
With hopes and fears, and joys with sorrows mixed.

The next returning planetary hour
Of Mars, who shared the heptarchy of power,
His steps bold Arcite to the temple bent,
To adore with pagan rites the power armipotent:
Then prostrate low before his altar lay,
And raised his manly voice, and thus began to pray:
"Strong God of Arms! whose iron scepter sways
The freezing north and Hyperborean seas,
And Scythian colds, and Thracia's wintry coast,
Where stand thy steeds, and thou art honored most:
There most; but everywhere thy power is known,
The fortune of the fight is all thy own:
Terror is thine, and wild amazement, flung
From out thy chariot, withers e'en the strong;
And disarray and shameful rout ensue,
And force is added to the fainting crew.
Acknowledged as thou art, accept my prayer:
If aught I have achieved deserve thy care;
If to my utmost power, with sword and shield,
I dared the death, unknowing how to yield;
And falling in my rank, still kept the field:
Then let my arm prevail, by thee sustained,
That Emily by conquest may be gained.
Have pity on my pains; nor those unknown
To Mars, which, when a lover, were his own.
By those dear pleasures, aid my arms in fight,
And make me conquer in my patron's right:

For I am young, a novice in the trade,
The fool of love, unpractised to persuade;
And she I love or laughs at all my pain
Or knows her worth too well, and pays me with
disdain.
For sure I am, unless I win in arms,
To stand excluded from Emilia's charms:
Nor can my strength avail, unless by thee
Endued with force, I gain the victory:
Then for the fire which warmed thy generous heart,
Pity thy subject's pains and equal smart:
So be the morrow's sweat and labor mine;
The palm and honor of the conquest thine.
Then shall the war, and stern debate, and strife
Immortal, be the business of my life;
And in thy fane, the dusty spoils among,
High on the burnished roof my banner shall be
hung,
Ranked with my champion's bucklers, and below,
With arms reversed, the achievements[1] of my foe:
And while these limbs the vital spirit feeds,
While day to night, and night to day succeeds,
Thy smoking altars shall be fat with food
Of incense, and the grateful steam of blood;
Burnt offerings morn and evening shall be thine,
And fires eternal in thy temple shine.
The bush of yellow beard, this length of hair,
Which from my birth inviolate I bear,
Guiltless of steel, and from the razor free,
Shall fall, a plenteous crop, reserved for thee.
So may my arms with victory be blest,
I ask no more, let fate dispose the rest."

[1] Shield.

The champion ceased: there followed in the close
A hollow groan; a murmuring wind arose;
The rings of iron that on the doors were hung
Sent out a jarring sound, and harshly rung;
The bolted gates flew open at the blast;
The storm rushed in; and Arcite stood aghast;
The flames were blown aside, yet shone they bright,
Fanned by the wind, and gave a ruffled light.

Then from the ground a scent began to rise,
Sweet smelling, as accepted sacrifice:
This omen pleased; and as the flames aspire,
With odorous incense Arcite heaps the fire;
Nor wanted hymns to Mars, or heathen charms;
At length the nodding statue clashed his arms,
And with a sullen sound and feeble cry,
Half sunk and half pronounced the word of victory!
For this, with soul devout, he thanked the god;
And, of success secure, returned to his abode.

These vows, thus granted, raised a strife above,
Betwixt the God of War and Queen of Love.
She, granting first, had right of time to plead;
But he had granted too, nor would recede.
Jove was for Venus, but he feared his wife,
And seemed unwilling to decide the strife;
Till Saturn from his leaden throne arose,
And found a way the difference to compose:
Though sparing of his grace, to mischief bent,
He seldom does a good with good intent.
Wayward, but wise; by long experience taught;
To please both parties, for ill ends, he sought:

For this advantage age from youth has won,
As not to be outridden, though outrun.
"Cease, daughter, to complain, and stint[1] the strife;
Thy Palamon shall have his promised wife;
And Mars, the lord of conquest, in the fight
With palm and laurel shall adorn his knight.
Wide is my course, nor turn I to my place
Till length of time, and move with tardy pace.
Man feels me when I press the ethereal plains;
My hand is heavy, and the wound remains.
Mine is the shipwreck, in a watery sign;
And in an earthy, the dark dungeon mine.
Cold shivering agues, melancholy care,
And bitter blasting winds, and poisoned air,
Are mine; and wilful death, resulting from despair.
The throttling quinsy 'tis my star appoints,
And rheumatisms I send, to rack the joints.
When churls rebel against their native prince,
I arm their hands, and furnish the pretense;
And housing in the Lion's hateful sign,
Bought senates and deserting troops are mine.
Mine is the privy poisoning; I command
Unkindly seasons and ungrateful land;
By me kings' palaces are pushed to ground,
And miners crushed beneath their mines are found;
'Twas I slew Samson, when the pillared hall
Fell down, and crushed the many with the fall.
My looking is the sire of pestilence,
That sweeps at once the people and the prince.
Now weep no more, but trust thy grandsire's art;
Mars shall be pleased, and thou perform thy part.
'Tis ill, though different your complexions are,

[1] Give over.

The family of heaven for men should war."
The expedient pleased, where neither lost his right:
Mars had the day, and Venus had the night.
The management they left to Chronos' care;
Now turn we to the effect, and sing the war.

PART V

In Athens all was pleasure, mirth, and play,
All proper to the Spring and sprightly May;
Which every soul inspired with such delight,
'Twas jousting all the day, and love at night.
Heaven smiled, and gladdened was the heart of man;
And Venus had the world as when it first began.
At length in sleep their bodies they compose,
And dreamt the future fight, and early rose.

Now scarce the dawning day began to spring,
As, at a signal given, the streets with clamors ring:
At once the crowd arose; confused and high,
Even from the heavens was heard a shouting cry,
For Mars was early up, and roused the sky.
The gods came downward to behold the wars,
Sharpening their sights, and leaning from their stars.
The neighing of the generous horse was heard,
For battle by the busy groom prepared:
Rustling of harness, rattling of the shield,
Clattering of armor furbished for the field.
Crowds to the castle mounted up the street,
Battering the pavement with their coursers' feet:
The greedy sight might there devour the gold
Of glittering arms, too dazzling to behold;

And polished steel, that cast the view aside,
And crested morions[1] with their plumy pride.
Knights, with a long retinue of their squires,
In gaudy liveries march, and quaint attires.
One laced the helm, another held the lance,
A third the shining buckler did advance.
The courser pawed the ground with restless feet,
And snorting foamed, and champed the golden bit.
The smiths and armorers on palfreys ride,
Files in their hands, and hammers at their side,
And nails for loosened spears, and thongs for shields
provide.
The yeomen guard the streets in seemly bands,
And clowns come crowding on with cudgels in their
hands.

The trumpets, next the gate in order placed,
Attend[2] the sign to sound the martial blast;
The palace yard is filled with floating tides,
And the last comers bear the former to the sides.
The throng is in the midst; the common crew
Shut out, the hall admits the better few.
In knots they stand, or in a rank they walk,
Serious in aspect, earnest in their talk;
Factious, and favoring this or t'other side,
As their strong fancies and weak reason guide.
Their wagers back their wishes; numbers hold
With the fair freckled king, and beard of gold;
So vigorous are his eyes, such rays they cast,
So prominent his eagle's beak is placed.
But most their looks on the black monarch bend,
His rising muscles and his brawn commend;

[1] Helmets.
[2] Await.

His double-biting axe and beamy spear,
Each asking a gigantic force to rear.
All spoke as partial favor moved the mind,
And, safe themselves, at others' cost divined.
Waked by the cries, the Athenian chief arose,
The knightly forms of combat to dispose,
And passing through the obsequiou guards, he sate
Conspicuous on a throne, sublime in state.
There, for the two contending knights he sent;
Armed cap-a-pie, with reverence low they bent;
He smiled on both, and with superior look
Alike their offered adoration took.
The people press on every side to see
Their awful prince, and hear his high decree.
Then signing to their heralds with his hand,
They gave his orders from their lofty stand.
Silence is thrice enjoined; then thus aloud
The king at arms bespeaks the knights and listening
crowd:

"Our sovereign lord has pondered in his mind
The means to spare the blood of gentle kind;
And of his grace and inborn clemency,
He modifies his first severe decree.
The keener edge of battle to rebate,
The troops for honor fighting, not for hate,
He wills, not death should terminate their strife;
And wounds, if wounds ensue, be short of life;
But issues, ere the fight, his dread command,
That slings afar, and poniards hand to hand,
Be banished from the field; that none shall dare
With shortened sword to stab in closer war;

But in fair combat fight with manly strength;
Nor push with biting point, but strike at length.
The tourney is allowed but one career
Of the tough ash with the sharp-grinded spear:
But knights unhorsed may rise from off the plain,
And fight on foot their honor to regain.
Nor, if at mischief taken, on the ground
Be slain, but prisoners to the pillar bound,
At either barrier placed; nor, captives made,
Be freed; or, armed anew, the fight invade.
The chief of either side bereft of life,
Or yielded to his foe, concludes the strife.
Thus dooms the lord: now, valiant knights and young,
Fight each his fill with swords and maces long."

The herald ends; the vaulted firmament
With loud acclaims and vast applause is rent:
"Heaven guard a prince so gracious and so good,
So just, and yet so provident of blood!"
This was the general cry. The trumpet's sound
And warlike symphony is heard around.
The marching troops through Athens take their way,
The great earl-marshal orders their array.
The casements are with golden tissue spread,
And horses' hoofs, for earth, on silken tapestry tread.
The king goes midmost, and the rivals ride
In equal rank, and close his either side.
Next after these, there rode the royal wife,
With Emily, the cause and the reward of strife.
The following cavalcade, by three and three,
Proceed by titles marshaled in degree.
Thus through the southern gate they take their way,

And at the lists arrived ere prime of day.
There, parting from the king, the chiefs divide,
And wheeling east and west, before their meiny[1] ride.
The Athenian monarch mounts his throne on high,
And after him the queen, and Emily:
Next these, the kindred of the crown are graced
With nearer seats, and lords by ladies placed.
Scarce were they seated, when with clamors loud
In rushed at once a rude promiscuous crowd;
The guards and then each other overbear,
And in a moment throng the spacious theater.
Now changed the jarring noise to whispers low,
As winds forsaking seas more softly blow,
When at the western gate, on which the car
Is placed aloft that bears the God of War,
Proud Arcite, entering armed before his train,
Stops at the barrier and divides the plain;
Red was his banner, and displayed abroad
The bloody colors of his patron god.

At that self-moment enters Palamon
The gate of Venus and the rising sun;
Waved by the wanton winds, his banner flies,
All maiden white, and shares the people's eyes
From east to west, look all the world around,
Two troops so matched were never to be found;
Such bodies built for strength, of equal age,
In stature sized; so proud an equipage:
The nicest eye could no distinction make,
Where lay the advantage, or what side to take.
Thus ranged, the herald for the last proclaims
A silence, while they answered to their names:

[1] Attendant companies.

For so the king decreed, to shun with care
The fraud of musters false, the common bane of war.
The tale was just,[1] and then the gates were closed;
And chief to chief, and troop to troop opposed.
The heralds last retired and loudly cried,
"The fortune of the field be fairly tried!"

At this, the challenger with fierce defy
His trumpet sounds; the challenged makes reply;
With clangor rings the field, resounds the vaulted sky.
Their vizors closed, their lances in the rest,
Or at the helmet pointed, or the crest;
They vanish from the barrier, speed the race,
And spurring see decrease the middle space.
A cloud of smoke envelops either host,
And all at once the combatants are lost:
Darkling they join adverse, and shock unseen,
Coursers with coursers jostling, men with men:
As laboring in eclipse, awhile they stay,
Till the next blast of wind restores the day.
They look anew: the beauteous form of fight
Is changed, and war appears a grisly sight.
Two troops in fair array one moment showed,
The next, a field with fallen bodies strowed:
Not half the number in their seats are found;
But men and steeds lie groveling on the ground.
The points of spears are stuck within the shield,
The steeds without their riders scour the field.
The knights, unhorsed, on foot renew the fight;
The glittering falchions cast a gleaming light:
Hauberks and helms are hewed with many a wound;
Out spins the streaming blood, and dyes the ground.

[1] The count was correct.

The mighty maces with such haste descend,
They break the bones, and make the solid armor
bend.
This thrusts amid the throng with furious force;
Down goes, at once, the horseman and the horse:
That courser stumbles on the fallen steed,
And, floundering, throws the rider o'er his head.
One rolls along, a football to his foes;
One with a broken truncheon deals his blows.
This halting, this disabled with his wound,
In triumph led, is to the pillar bound,
Where, by the king's award, he must abide:
There goes a captive led on the other side.
By fits they cease; and leaning on the lance
Take breath a while; and to new fight
advance.
Full oft the rivals met, and neither spared
His utmost force, and each forgot to ward.
The head of this was to the saddle bent,
That other backward to the crupper sent;
Both were by turns unhorsed; the jealous blows
Fall thick and heavy, when on foot they close.
So deep their falchions bite, that every stroke
Pierced to the quick; and equal wounds they gave
and took.
Borne far asunder by the tides of men,
Like adamant and steel they meet again.
So when a tiger sucks the bullock's blood,
A famished lion issuing from the wood
Roars lordly fierce, and challenges the food;
Each claims possession, neither will obey,
But both their paws are fastened on the prey:

They bite, they tear; and while in vain they strive,
The swains come armed between, and both to distance
drive.

At length, as fate foredoomed, and all things tend
By course of time to their appointed end;
So when the sun to west was far declined,
And both afresh in mortal battle joined,
The strong Emetrius came in Arcite's aid,
And Palamon with odds was overlaid:
For turning short, he struck with all his might
Full on the helmet of the unwary knight.
Deep was the wound; he staggered with the blow,
And turned him to his unexpected foe;
Whom with such force he struck, he felled him down,
And cleft the circle of his golden crown.
But Arcite's men, who now prevailed in fight,
Twice ten at once surround the single knight:
O'erpowered at length, they force him to the ground,
Unyielded as he was, and to the pillar bound;
And King Lycurgus, while he fought in vain
His friend to free, was tumbled on the plain.

Who now laments but Palamon, compelled
No more to try the fortune of the field!
And worse than death, to view with hateful[1] eyes
His rival's conquest, and renounce the prize!

The royal judge on his tribunal placed,
Who had beheld the fight from first to last,
Bade cease the war; pronouncing from on high
Arcite of Thebes had won the beauteous Emily.

[1] Full of hate.

The sound of trumpets to the voice replied,
And round the royal lists the heralds cried,
"Arcite of Thebes has won the beauteous bride."

The people rend the skies with vast applause;
All own the chief, when fortune owns the cause.
But Venus with dejected eyes appears,
And weeping on the lists distilled her tears;
Her will refused, which grieves a woman most,
And in her champion foiled, the cause of love is lost.
Till Saturn said, "Fair daughter, now be still,
The blustering fool has satisfied his will;
His boon is given; his knight has gained the day,
But lost the prize; the arrears are yet to pay.
Thy hour is come, and mine the care shall be
To please thy knight, and set thy promise free."

Now while the heralds run the lists around,
And "Arcite, Arcite," heaven and earth resound;
A miracle (nor less it could be called)
Their joy with unexpected sorrow palled.
The victor-knight had laid his helm aside,
Part for his ease, the greater part for pride;
Bareheaded, popularly low he bowed,
And paid the salutations of the crowd.
Then spurring at full speed, ran endlong on
Where Theseus sate on his imperial throne;
Furious he drove, and upward cast his eye,
Where next the queen was placed his Emily;
Then passing, to the saddle-bow he bent;
A sweet regard the gracious virgin lent:
(For women, to the brave an easy prey,

Still follow fortune, where she leads the way)
Just then, from earth sprung out a flashing fire,
By Pluto sent, at Saturn's bad desire:
The startling steed was seized with sudden fright,
And, bounding, o'er the pommel cast the knight:
Forward he flew, and pitching on his head,
He quivered with his feet, and lay for dead.
Black was his countenance in a little space,
For all the blood was gathered in his face.
Help was at hand; they reared him from the ground,
And from his cumbrous arms[1] his limbs unbound;
Then lanced a vein, and watched returning breath;
It came, but clogged with symptoms of his death.
The saddle-bow the noble parts had pressed,
All bruised and mortified his manly breast.
Him still entranced, and in a litter laid,
They bore from field, and to his bed conveyed.
At length he waked, and with a feeble cry,
The word he first pronounced was "Emily."

Meantime the king, though inwardly he mourned,
In pomp triumphant to the town returned,
Attended by the chiefs, who fought the field;
(Now friendly mixed, and in one troop compelled.)
Composed his looks to counterfeited cheer,
And bade them not for Arcite's life to fear.
But that which gladdened all the warrior-train,
Though most were sorely wounded, none were slain.
The surgeons soon despoiled 'em of their arms,
And some with salves they cure, and some with
 charms;
Foment the bruises, and the pains assuage,

[1] Armor.

And heal their inward hurts with sovereign draughts of
sage.
The king in person visits all around,
Comforts the sick, congratulates the sound;
Honors the princely chiefs, rewards the rest,
And holds for thrice three days a royal feast.
None was disgraced; for falling is no shame;
And cowardice alone is loss of fame.
The venturous knight is from the saddle thrown;
But 'tis the fault of fortune, not his own.
If crowns and palms the conquering side adorn,
The victor under better stars was born:
The brave man seeks not popular applause,
Nor, overpowered with arms, deserts his cause;
Unshamed, though foiled, he does the best he can;
Force is of brutes, but honor is of man.

Thus Theseus smiled on all with equal grace;
And each was set according to his place.
With ease were reconciled the different parts,
For envy never dwells in noble hearts.
At length they took their leave, the time expired,
Well pleased; and to their several homes retired.

Meanwhile the health of Arcite still impairs;
From bad proceeds to worse, and mocks the leeches'
cares:
Swollen in his breast, his inward pains increase,
All means are used, and all without success.
The clotted blood lies heavy on his heart,
Corrupts, and there remains in spite of art:
Nor breathing veins, nor cupping will prevail;

All outward remedies and inward fail:
The mould of Nature's fabric is destroyed,
Her vessels discomposed, her virtue void:
The bellows of his lungs begin to swell:
All out of frame is every secret cell,
Nor can the good receive, nor bad expel.
Those breathing organs, thus within oppressed,
With venom soon distend the sinews of his breast.
The midmost region battered and destroyed,
When Nature cannot work, the effect of art is void;
For physic can but mend our crazy state,
Patch an old building, not a new create.
Arcite is doomed to die in all his pride,
Must leave his youth, and yield his beauteous bride,
Gained hardly, against right, and unenjoyed.
When 'twas declared all hope of life was past,
Conscience (that of all physic works the last)
Caused him to send for Emily in haste.
With her, at his desire, came Palamon;
Then, on his pillow raised, he thus begun:

"No language can express the smallest part
Of what I feel and suffer in my heart
For you, whom best I love and value most:
But to your service I bequeath my ghost;
Which from this mortal body when untied,
Unseen, unheard, shall hover at your side;
Vain men, how vanishing a bliss we crave,
Now warm in love, now withering in the grave!
Farewell! but take me dying in your arms,
'Tis all I can enjoy of all your charms:
This hand I cannot but in death resign;

Ah, could I live! but while I live 'tis mine.
So help me Heaven! in all the world is none
So worthy to be loved as Palamon.
He loves you too with such a holy fire,
As will not, can not, but with life expire:
If e'er you plight your vows when I am gone,
Have pity on the faithful Palamon!"

This was his last; for death came on amain,
And exercised below his iron reign;
Then upward, to the seat of life he goes;
Sense fled before him, what he touched he froze;
Yet could he not his closing eyes withdraw,
Though less and less of Emily he saw;
So speechless for a little space he lay,
Then grasped the hand he held, and sighed his soul
away.
But whither went his soul, let such relate
Who search the secrets of the future state:
Divines can say but what themselves believe;
Strong proofs they have, but not demonstrative;
For, were all plain, then all sides must agree,
And faith itself be lost in certainty.
To live uprightly then is surely best,
To save ourselves, and not to damn the rest.
The soul of Arcite went where heathens go,
Who better live than we, though less they know.

In Palamon a manly grief appears;
Silent he wept, ashamed to show his tears:
Emilia shrieked but once, and then, oppressed
With sorrow, sunk upon her lover's breast.

The face of things is changed, and Athens now,
That laughed so late, becomes the scene of woe:
Matrons and maids, both sexes, every state,
With tears lament the knight's untimely fate.
Not greater grief in falling Troy was seen
For Hector's death; but Hector was not then.
Old men with dust deformed their hoary hair,
The women beat their breasts, their cheeks they tear.
"Why would'st thou go," (with one consent they cry)
"When thou had'st gold enough, and Emily?"
Theseus himself, who should have cheered the grief
Of others, wanted now the same relief.
Old Egeus only could revive his son,
Who various changes of the world had known,
And strange vicissitudes of human fate,
Still altering, never in a steady state;
Good after ill, and after pain delight;
Alternate, like the scenes of day and night.
"Since every man who lives is born to die,
And none can boast sincere felicity,
With equal mind what happens let us bear,
Nor joy nor grieve too much for things beyond our care.
Like pilgrims to the appointed place we tend;
The world's an inn, and death the journey's end.
Even kings but play; and when their part is done,
Some other, worse or better, mount the throne."
With words like these the crowd was satisfied,
And so they would have been, had Theseus died.

But he, their king, was laboring in his mind,
A fitting place for funeral pomps to find,

Which were in honor of the dead designed.
And after long debate, at last he found
(As love itself had marked the spot of ground)
That grove forever green, that conscious land,
Where he with Palamon fought hand to hand:
That where he fed his amorous desires
With soft complaints, and felt his hottest fires;
There other flames might waste his earthly part,
And burn his limbs, where love had burned his heart.

This once resolved, the peasants were enjoined
Sere wood, and firs, and doddered[1] oaks to find.
With sounding axes to the grove they go,
Fell, split, and lay the fuel on a row,
Vulcanian food: a bier is next prepared,
On which the lifeless body should be reared,
Covered with cloth of gold, on which was laid
The corpse of Arcite, in like robes arrayed.
White gloves were on his hands, and on his head
A wreath of laurel, mixed with myrtle, spread.
A sword keen-edged within his right he held,
The warlike emblem of the conquered field:
Bare was his manly visage on the bier;
Menaced his countenance, even in death severe.
Then to the palace hall they bore the knight,
To lie in solemn state, a public sight.
Groans, cries, and howlings fill the crowded place,
And unaffected sorrow sat on every face.
Sad Palamon above the rest appears,
In sable garments, dewed with gushing tears;
His auburn locks on either shoulder flowed,
Which to the funeral of his friend he vowed;

[1] Ready to fall.

But Emily, as chief, was next his side,
A virgin-widow, and a mourning bride.
And that the princely obsequies might be
Performed according to his high degree,
The steed that bore him living to the fight
Was trapped with polished steel, all shining bright,
And covered with the achievements[1] of the knight.
The riders rode abreast, and one his shield,
His lance of cornel-wood another held;
The third his bow; and, glorious to behold,
The costly quiver, all of burnished gold.
The noblest of the Grecians next appear,
And, weeping, on their shoulders bore the bier;
With sober pace they marched, and often stayed,
And through the master-street the corpse conveyed.
The houses to their tops with black were spread,
And even the pavements were with mourning hid.
The right side of the pall old Egeus kept,
And on the left the royal Theseus wept;
Each bore a golden bowl of work divine,
With honey filled and milk, and mixed with ruddy
wine;
Then Palamon, the kinsman of the slain,
And after him appeared the illustrious train:
To grace the pomp, came Emily the bright,
With covered fire, the funeral pile to light.

With high devotion was the service made,
And all the rites of pagan honor paid:
So lofty was the pile, a Parthian bow,
With vigor drawn, must send the shaft below.
The bottom was full twenty fathom broad,

[1] Armorial bearings.

With crackling straw beneath in due proportion
strowed.
The fabric seemed a wood of rising green,
With sulphur and bitumen cast between
To feed the flames: the trees were unctuous fir,
And mountain-ash, the mother of the spear;
The mourner yew, and builder oak were there,
The beech, the swimming alder, and the plane,
Hard box, and linden of a softer grain,
And laurels, which the gods for conquering chiefs
ordain.
How they were ranked, shall rest untold by me,
With nameless nymphs that lived in every tree;
Nor how the dryads, and the woodland train,
Disherited, ran howling o'er the plain:
Nor how the birds to foreign seats repaired,
Or beasts, that bolted out, and saw the forest bared:
Nor how the ground, now cleared, with ghastly fright
Beheld the sudden sun, a stranger to the light.
The straw, as first I said, was laid below;
Of chips and sere-wood was the second row;
The third of greens, and timber newly felled;
The fourth high stage the fragrant odors held,
And pearls, and precious stones, and rich array;
In midst of which, embalmed, the body lay.
The service sung, the maid with mourning eyes
The stubble fired; the smouldering flames arise;
This office done, she sunk upon the ground;
But what she spoke, recovered from her swound,
I want the wit in moving words to dress;
But by themselves the tender sex may guess.
While the devouring fire was burning fast,

Rich jewels in the flame the wealthy cast;
And some their shields, and some their lances threw,
And gave their warrior's ghost a warrior's due.
Full bowls of wine, of honey, milk, and blood,
Were poured upon the pile of burning wood,
And hissing flames receive, and hungry lick the food.
Then thrice the mounted squadrons ride around
The fire, and Arcite's name they thrice resound:
"Hail! and farewell!" they shouted thrice amain,
Thrice facing to the left, and thrice they turned again;
Still as they turned, they beat their clattering shields;
The women mix their cries; and clamor fills the fields.
The warlike wakes continued all the night,
And funeral games were played at new returning light;
Who naked wrestled best, besmeared with oil,
Or who with gauntlets gave or took the foil,
I will not tell you, nor would you attend;
But briefly haste to my long story's end.

I pass the rest; the year was fully mourned,
And Palamon long since to Thebes returned,
When by the Grecians' general consent,
At Athens Theseus held his parliament:
Among the laws that passed, it was decreed
That conquered Thebes from bondage should be freed;
Reserving homage to the Athenian throne,
To which the sovereign summoned Palamon.
Unknowing of the cause, he took his way,
Mournful in mind, and still in black array.

The monarch mounts the throne, and placed on high,
Commands into the court the beauteous Emily:

So called, she came; the senate rose, and paid
Becoming reverence to the royal maid.
And first, soft whispers through the assembly went;
With silent wonder then they watched the event:
All hushed, the king arose with awful grace,
Deep thought was in his breast, and counsel in his face.

At length he sighed; and having first prepared
The attentive audience, thus his will declared:

"The Cause and Spring of motion, from above
Hung down on earth the golden chain of love:
Great was the effect, and high was his intent,
When peace among the jarring seeds he sent.
Fire, flood, and earth, and air, by this were bound,
And love, the common link, the new creation crowned.
The chain still holds; for though the forms decay,
Eternal matter never wears away:
The same First Mover certain bounds has placed,
How long those perishable forms shall last;
Nor can they last beyond the time assigned
By that all-seeing and all-making Mind:
Shorten their hours they may, for will is free,
But never pass the appointed destiny.
Then since those forms begin, and have their end,
On some unaltered Cause they sure depend:
Parts of the whole are we, but God the whole,
Who gives us life, and animating soul.
For nature can not from a part derive
That being, which the whole can only give:
He perfect, stable; but imperfect we,
Subject to change, and different in degree;

Plants, beasts, and man, and, as our organs are,
We more or less of his perfection share.
But by a long descent, the ethereal fire
Corrupts; and forms, the mortal part, expire:
As he withdraws his virtue, so they pass,
And the same matter makes another mass.
This law the omniscient Power was pleased to give,
That every kind should by succession live:
That individuals die, His will ordains;
The propagated species still remains.
The monarch oak, the patriarch of the trees,
Shoots rising up, and spreads by slow degrees;
Three centuries he grows, and three he stays
Supreme in state, and in three more decays;
So wears the paving pebble in the street,
And towns and towers their fatal periods meet:
So rivers, rapid once, now naked lie,
Forsaken of their springs, and leave their channels dry.
Then 'tis our best, since thus ordained to die,
To make a virtue of necessity.
And could we choose the time, and choose aright,
'Tis best to die, our honor at the height,
When we have done our ancestors no shame,
But served our friends, and well secured our fame.
Then should we wish our happy life to close,
And leave no more for fortune to dispose:
So should we make our death a glad relief
From future shame, from sickness, and from grief:
Enjoying, while we live, the present hour,
And dying in our excellence and flower.
Then round our death-bed every friend should run,
And joy us of our conquest, early won:

While the malicious world with envious tears
Should grudge our happy end, and wish it theirs.
Since then our Arcite is with honor dead,
Why should we mourn, that he so soon is freed,
Or call untimely what the gods decreed?
With grief as just, a friend may be deplored
From a foul prison to free air restored.
Ought he to thank his kinsman, or his wife,
Could tears recall him into wretched life?
Their sorrow hurts themselves; on him is lost;
And worse than both, offends his happy ghost.
What then remains, but after past annoy,
To take the good vicissitude of joy?
To thank the gracious gods for what they give;
Possess our souls, and while we live, to live?
Ordain we then two sorrows to combine,

Chaucer's Dwelling

And in one point the extremes of grief to join,
That, thence resulting, joy may be renewed,
As jarring notes in harmony conclude.
Then I propose, that Palamon shall be
In marriage joined with beauteous Emily;
For which already I have gained the assent
Of my free people in full parliament.
Long love to her has borne the faithful knight,
And well deserved, had Fortune done him right:
'Tis time to mend her fault; since Emily
By Arcite's death from former vows is free.
If you, fair sister, ratify the accord,
And take him for your husband and your lord,
'Tis no dishonor to confer your grace
On one descended from a royal race:
And were he less, yet years of service past
From grateful souls exact reward at last:
Pity is heaven's and yours: nor can she find
A throne so soft as in a woman's mind."

He said; she blushed; and as o'erawed by might,
Seemed to give Theseus what she gave the knight.
Then turning to the Theban thus he said:
"Small arguments are needful to persuade
Your temper to comply with my command;"
And speaking thus, he gave Emilia's hand.
Smiled Venus, to behold her own true knight
Obtain the conquest, though he lost the fight.
All of a tenor was their after-life,
No day discolored with domestic strife;
No jealousy, but mutual truth believed,
Secure repose, and kindness undeceived.

"Now endeth Palamon and Emily,
And God save all this gracious company!"
Thus closed the Knight the tale that he had told,
And in our troop was no one, young or old,
Who did not say it was a noble story,
Well worthy of remembrance and of glory,
Especially the gentles every one.

Our Host laughed out and swore: " 'Tis well begun.
Unbuckled is the bag that holds the mail.
Let see now who shall tell another tale,
For verily the game is under way.
And now, Sir Monk, relate, if so ye may,
Something to match the Knight's full joyous tale."

The Miller, who already was all pale
For drunkenness so that he hardly sat
Upon his horse, would doff nor hood nor hat,
Nor stay his speech for any courtesy,
But in a blustering voice began to cry,
Swearing by arms and legs and bones and blood:
"I know a noble tale, a tale so good
'Twill match the Knight's. I next will tell a tale."

Our Host, who saw that he was drunk of ale,
Said: "Bide thy turn; bide, Robin, dear my
brother;
Some better man shall tell us first another.
Let's work by my decrees and by the lot."

"Now by my soul," quoth he, "that will I not;
For I will speak, or else the train I quit."

The Miller

"Then tell thy tale, thou fool, bad luck to it!"
Answered our Host. "Thy brains are overcome."

"Now hearken," quoth the Miller, "all and some.
But first that I am drunk I bid you note.
I wot it by the thickness in my throat.
So if I stutter or my words miscall,
Blame you the ale of Southwark for it all.
For I will tell a legend, on my life,
Both of a carpenter and of his wife,
And of an Oxford scholar gay and young."

The Steward

Then spake the Steward: "Hold thy drunken tongue."
[For the Steward was a carpenter by craft,
And of his shrewdness deemed that tale might graft
Shame on a carpenter, as sooth it did,
So if I pass it, need I not be chid.
'Twas a clown's tale and told in clownish sort.
Most of the pilgrims laughed and took in sport
Both tale and teller, save for three or four,
The Knight, the Clerk, the Parson, who forebore
To praise it, and the Nuns their veils drew close;
But the only man aggrieved was that morose
Oswold, the Steward, whose white top declared
His years were old, yet still a red flame flared
In the ashes of his heart. He needs must rail

Upon the Miller and the Miller's tale.
Of doleful age and death he spake anon,
And how the tap of life is quickly gone,
And naught but wretchedness a man hath won,
For all is vanity, saith Solomon.]

But our Host, when he had heard this sermoning,
Began to speak as lordly as a king.
He said: "To what amounteth all this wit?
What! shall we prate all day of Holy Writ?
As well, forsooth, may cobbler turn a leech,
As steward take upon himself to preach.
Speak out thy tale; get with the Miller even;
But tarry not, for it is half-past seven.
We are at Greenwich—'tis a town wherein
Are many shrews (like mine)—; thy tale begin."

"Now, sirs," Oswold the Steward quoth, "I pray
'Twill be no blemish on your holiday
If I the Miller's impudence outjest,
For cudgel is by cudgel answered best.
He told us how an Oxford clerk—more shame
To scholars!—of a carpenter made game,
Perchance in scorn of me, for I am one,
But I'll be quits with him ere day is done.
Of clownish terms like his my tale I'll make.
I would the reeling rogue his neck might break.
Within mine eye he spies a mote, 'twould seem,
But in his own he cannot see a beam."
[Therewith the Steward told a story base,
That made the gentles ride at quicker pace
And leave it out of hearing. It cast scorn

Upon a Miller, thief of meal and corn,
Who by a pair of Cambridge clerks he swore
To rob, himself was robbed and beaten sore.
And thus the Steward ended:] "Thence we learn
Those who do ill must look for ill return.
Beguilers shall themselves beguilèd be.
And God, that sitteth high in Trinity,
Save all this fellowship! With quip and scoff
Now has my story paid the Miller off."

The Cook

The London Cook, while thus the Steward spoke,
Clawed him upon the back for joy. "Good joke
Was that," quoth he. "Let's keep the ball in air.
And if your honorable worships care
To hear a tale of me, so poor a man,

I will you tell, as well as ever I can,
A prank was played in our own London city.''

Our Host replied: "I grant it, but 'twere pity
If this thy tale should prove as little tasty
As many a mess of thine in pie and pasty;
For, Roger, many a pudding hast thou sold
That has been two times hot and two times cold.
Thy parsley has had many a pilgrim's curse,
Because for it they feel them still the worse,
That parsley eaten with thy tough gray goose.
Within thy shop full many a fly goes loose.
Tell on now, gentle Roger by thy name,
But be not wroth for what I said in game,
Though man may speak the truth in game and play."

Quoth Roger: "Let the truth be as it may,
True jest is bad jest, as the Fleming saith,
And therefore, Harry Bailly, by thy faith
Be thou not wroth if, ere our journey's done,
I tell a tale holds landlords up to fun.
But not yet on it will I try my wits,
Though, ere we part, that tale shall see us quits.''
And therewithal he laughed and made good cheer
And told his tale as ye shall after hear.
[The tale was of a prentice, young and merry,
A reveler, as brown as any berry,
Tuneful as goldfinch when the days are sunny,
His heart as full of love as hive of honey,
Yet such an idle, wasteful, reckless fellow,
Soon was his green leaf blighted into yellow.
But hardly was this story under way

When Chaucer dropt it to resume some day
That never dawned for him; nor did he tell
How wore that afternoon, how evening fell,
Nor where they lodged that night, though scholars say
It was at Dartford, fifteen miles away
From London, for so many folk together
Would ride but slowly through the April weather.]

THE SECOND DAY

[When next the Poet, on whose grace we wait,
Shows us the train of pilgrims, waxen late
The April morning was; refreshed and glad
They cantered on and many a Godspeed had
From folk along the way, who guessed their tryst,
Pages afield with falcon on the wrist,
Archers at gaze, forgetful of the score,
And grandams sunning in the cottage door;
And laughing lads, if boys were then as now,
Ran with the troop a space, or from some bough
That overhung the highroad, slyly sent
A rain of blossoms on them as they went.
But when the even shadow of the trees
Told ten o'clock, our Host rebuked our ease.]
He reined his horse up suddenly and cried:
"Gentles, I warn you all, as here you ride,
A quarter portion of this day is gone.
Now for the love of God and of Saint John,
Lose time no more, redeem it while ye may.
Gentles, the time is slipping night and day
And stealeth from us—what with the hours that flow
In sleep or we by negligence let go—
As doth the stream that turneth never again,
Descending from the mountain to the plain.
Well might grave Seneca and sages hold
Lost time a weightier woe than stolen gold,
For 'loss of goods may yet recovered be,

Martyrdom of St. Thomas

But loss of time destroyeth us,' quoth he.
It will not come again for our redress.
Let us not moulder thus in idleness.
Sir Man of Law, now by your hope of bliss
Tell us a tale, as your agreement is.
Of your free will and choice you did engage
To do my bidding on this pilgrimage.
Hold by your compact, as a lawyer should.
Whate'er the tale, at least your word make
good."

"Mine Host," quoth he, "as lawyer I assent.
To break my promise is not mine intent.
Promise is debt, and I will do my best
To keep my word. For let it be confessed
What law man deals to others, by that law
He should himself abide,—but here's the flaw.
I cannot, though I would, a tale of worth
Relate to you, for somewhere on the earth
There walks—or rides—one Chaucer, who,
although
His meters are but lame, as all men know,
Has searched the world for stories, near and far,
And, with what wit he has, told all there are,
For if he has not told them, dear my brother,
In one book, he has told them in another,—
More tales of love than even Ovid knew;
What then, forsooth, is left for me to do?
I would not be as those rash maidens, who
Strove to outsing the Muses, and must rue
In magpie shape their folly evermore.[1]
But what care I though by his dainty store

[1] The Pierides.

The Man of Law

My fare be coarse? After the cream, the skim.
I speak in prose and leave the rhymes to him."
And with that word, he with a sober cheer
Began his tale, as ye shall after hear:
[Of Lady Constance then the tale he told,
Her beauty and her troubles manifold;
The daughter of an emperor was she,
And very mirror of all courtesy;
Her heart a chamber was of holiness,
And all her griefs did Christ her Saviour bless
Unto her peace eternal. Hushed with awe,
The pilgrims hearkened to this Man of Law,
Who thus closed up his story at the end:]
"Now Jesus Christ, that of His might may send
Joy after sorrow, guide us in His grace,
And keep from peril all within this place."

Our Host upon his stirrups stood anon
And said: "Good folk, attention, every one!
For all his fears, this was a tale of worth.
Sir Parish Priest," quoth he, "by heaven and earth,
Tell us a tale, as promise was of yore.
I see well that ye learnèd men of lore
Are good for something, by the God above."

The Parson answered: "Keep us in His love!
What aileth the man so sinfully to swear?"

The Host replied: "Oho! I have you there.
I smell a Lollard in the wind," quoth he,
"A heretic. Let all this company
Be on their guard, or by the Holy Cross,
Sir Solemn-Face, to our eternal loss,
Will preach a sermon to us on the spot."

"Nay, by my father's soul, that shall he not,"
The Sailor shouted. "Here he shall not preach,
Nor any dangerous new doctrine teach.
We all believe in the great God," quoth he.
"This Parson would but sow perplexity
Or sprinkle tares amid our honest corn.
And therefore, Host, your worship do I warn
My jolly body shall a story tell,
And I will tinkle you so merry a bell
That I shall waken all this company;
But it shall not be of philosophy
Nor physic nor of curious terms of law.
There is but little Latin in my maw."

The Shipman

[He told how that a monk by crafty plan
Cheated and robbed a thrifty merchant-man,
The merchant's wife assisting—sorry sport
To all the pilgrims but the baser sort.]

"Well said, man, by the Mass!" exclaimed our Host.
"Long may'st thou sail along our English coast,
Gentle Sir Skipper, gentle Mariner!
Loads of ill luck may such a monk incur!
Aha, my friends! beware of such a trick!
For all that merchant-man's arithmetic,
The monk a monkey made of him, I ween,
And his wife, too. Now by Saint Augustine,
Trust ye no monks. But pass we on and see
Who next of all this jocund company

Shall tell a tale." And with that word he said,
As courteously as to a fair young maid:
"My lady Prioress, by your good leave,
If I but wist that I should not you grieve,
I would give judgment that your soft voice should
Tell the next tale, if so were that ye would.
Now will you favor us, my lady dear?"
"Gladly," quoth she, and said as ye shall hear.

The Prioress

THE PRIORESS' TALE

I

O Lord, our Lord! how wondrously, (quoth she)
Thy name in this large world is spread abroad!
For not alone by men of dignity
Thy worship is performed and precious laud;
But by the mouths of children, gracious God!
Thy goodness is set forth; they when they lie
Upon the breast Thy name do glorify.

II

Wherefore in praise, the worthiest that I may
Jesu, of Thee, and the white Lily-flower
Which did Thee bear, and is a Maid for aye,
To tell a story I will use my power;
Not that I may increase her honor's dower,
For she herself is honor, and the root
Of goodness, next her Son, our soul's best boot.[1]

III

O Mother Maid! O Maid and Mother free!
O bush unburnt! burning in Moses' sight!
That down did'st ravish from the Deity,
Through humbleness, the spirit that did alight
Upon thy heart, whence, through that glory's
might,
Conceivèd was the Father's sapience,
Help me to tell it in thy reverence!

IV

Lady! thy goodness, thy magnificence,
Thy virtue, and thy great humility,
Surpass all science and all utterance;
For sometimes, Lady! ere men pray to thee
Thou goest before in thy benignity,
The light to us vouchsafing of thy prayer,
To be our guide unto thy Son so dear.

V

My knowledge is so weak, O blissful Queen!
To tell abroad thy mighty worthiness,
That I the weight of it may not sustain;
But as a child of twelve months old or less,
That laboreth his language to express,
Even so fare I; and therefore, I thee pray,
Guide thou my song which I of thee shall say.

1 Help.

VI

There was in Asia, in a mighty town,
'Mong Christian folk, a street where Jews might be,
Assigned to them and given them for their own
By a great Lord, for gain and usury,
Hateful to Christ and to his company;
And through this street who list might ride and wend;
Free was it, and unbarred at either end.

VII

A little school of Christian people stood
Down at the farther end, in which there were
A nest of children come of Christian blood,
That learnèd in that school from year to year
Such sort of doctrine as men usèd there,
That is to say, to sing, and read also,
As little children in their childhood do.

VIII

Among these children was a Widow's son,
A little scholar, scarcely seven years old,
Who day by day unto this school hath gone,
And eke, when he the image did behold
Of Jesu's Mother, as he had been told,
This Child was wont to kneel adown and say
Ave Maria, as he goeth by the way.

IX

This Widow thus her little Son hath taught
Our blissful Lady, Jesu's Mother dear,
To worship aye, and he forgat it not;
For simple infant hath a ready ear.
Sweet is the holiness of youth: and hence,
Calling to mind this matter when I may,
Saint Nicholas in my presence standeth aye,
For he so young to Christ did reverence.

X

This little Child, while in the school he sate
His Primer conning with an earnest cheer,
The whilst the rest their anthem-book repeat,
The *Alma Redemptoris* did he hear;
And as he durst he drew him near and near,
And hearkened to the words and to the note,
Till the first verse he learned it all by rote.

XI

This Latin knew he nothing what it said,
For he too tender was of age to know;
But to his comrade he repaired, and prayed
That he the meaning of this song would show,
And unto him declare why men sing so;
This oftentimes, that he might be at ease,
This Child did him beseech on his bare knees.

XII

His schoolfellow, who elder was than he,
Answered him thus:—"This song, I have heard say,
Was fashioned for our blissful Lady free;
Her to salute, and also her to pray
To be our help upon our dying day:
If there is more in this, I know it not;
Song do I learn,—small grammar I have got."

XIII

"And is this song fashioned in reverence
Of Jesu's Mother?" said this Innocent;
"Now, certès, I will use my diligence
To con it all ere Christmas-tide be spent;
Although I for my Primer shall be shent,[1]
And shall be beaten three times in an hour,
Our Lady I will praise with all my power."

[1] Punished.

XIV

His schoolfellow, whom he had so besought,
As they went homeward taught him privily,
And then he sang it well and fearlessly,
From word to word according to the note:
Twice in a day it passèd through his throat;
Homeward and schoolward whensoe'er he went,
On Jesu's Mother fixed was his intent.

XV

Through all the Jewry (this before said I)
This little Child, as he came to and fro,
Full merrily then would he sing and cry,
O Alma Redemptoris! high and low:
The sweetness of Christ's Mother piercèd so
His heart, that her to praise, to her to pray,
He cannot stop his singing by the way.

XVI

The Serpent, Satan, our first foe, that hath
His wasp's nest in Jew's heart, upswelled—"O woe!
O Hebrew people!" said he in his wrath,
"Is it an honest thing? Shall this be so?
That such a Boy where'er he lists shall go
In your despite, and sing his hymns and saws,[1]
Which is against the reverence of our laws!"

XVII

From that day forward have the Jews conspired
Out of the world this Innocent to chase;
And to this end a Homicide they hired,
That in an alley had a privy place,
And, as the Child 'gan to the school to pace,
This cruel Jew him seized, and held him fast
And cut his throat, and in a pit him cast.

[1] Texts.

XVIII

I say that him into a pit they threw,
A loathsome pit, whence noisome scents exhale;
A cursèd folk! away, ye Herods new!
What may your ill intentions you avail?
Murder will out; certes it will not fail;
Know, that the honor of high God may spread.
The blood cries out on your accursèd deed.

XIX

O Martyr 'stablished in virginity!
Now may'st thou sing for aye before the throne,
Following the Lamb celestial (quoth she),
Of which the great Evangelist, Saint John,
In Patmos wrote, who saith of them that go
Before the Lamb singing continually,
That never fleshly woman they did know.

XX

Now this poor widow waiteth all that night
After her little Child, and he came not;
For which, by earliest glimpse of morning light,
With face all pale with dread and busy thought,
She at the school and elsewhere him hath sought,
Until thus far she learned, that he had been
In the Jews' street, and there he last was seen.

XXI

With Mother's pity in her breast enclosed
She goeth, as she were half out of her mind,
To every place wherein she hath supposed
By likelihood her little Son to find;
And ever on Christ's Mother meek and kind
She cried, till to the Jewry she was brought,
And him among the accursèd Jews she sought.

XXII

She asketh, and she piteously doth pray
To every Jew that dwelleth in that place
To tell her if her child had passed that way;
They all said "Nay"; but Jesu of his grace
Gave to her thought, that in a little space
She for her Son in that same spot did cry
Where he was cast into a pit hard by.

XXIII

O thou great God that dost perform thy laud
By mouths of Innocents, lo! here thy might:
This gem of chastity, this emeraud,[1]
And eke of martyrdom this ruby bright,
There, where with mangled throat he lay upright,
The *Alma Redemptoris* 'gan to sing
So loud that with his voice the place did ring.

XXIV

The Christian folk that through the Jewry went,
Come to the spot in wonder at the thing;
And hastily they for the Provost sent;
Immediately he came, not tarrying,
And praiseth Christ that is our heavenly King,
And eke his Mother, honor of Mankind:
Which done, he bade that they the Jews should bind.

XXV

This Child with piteous lamentation then
Was taken up, singing his song alwày,
And with procession great and pomp of men
To the next Abbey him they bare away,
His Mother swooning by the body lay
And scarcely could the people that were near
Remove this second Rachel from the bier.

---

1 Emerald.

XXVI

Torment and shameful death to every one
This Provost doth for those bad Jews prepare
That of this murder wist, and that anon:
Such wickedness his judgments cannot spare;
Who will do evil, evil shall he bear;
Them therefore with wild horses did he draw,
And after that he hung them by the law.

XXVII

Upon his bier this Innocent doth lie
Before the altar while the Mass doth last:
The Abbot with his convent's company
Then sped themselves to bury him full fast;
And, when they holy water on him cast,
Yet spake this Child when sprinkled was the water,
And sang, *O Alma Redemptoris Mater!*

XXVIII

This Abbot, for he was a holy man,
As all Monks are, or surely ought to be,
In supplication to the Child began,
Thus saying, "O dear Child! I summon thee
In virtue of the holy Trinity
Tell me the cause why thou dost sing this hymn,
Since that thy throat is cut, as it doth seem."

XXIX

"My throat is cut into the bone, I trow,"
Said this young Child, "and by the law of kind[1]
I should have died, yea many hours ago;
But Jesus Christ, as in the books ye find,
Will that His glory last, and be in mind;
And, for the worship of His Mother dear,
Yet may I sing, *O Alma!* loud and clear.

[1] Nature.

XXX

"This well of mercy, Jesu's Mother sweet,
After my knowledge, I have loved alwày;
And in the hour when I my death did meet
To me she came, and thus to me did say:
'Thou in thy dying sing this holy lay,'
As ye have heard, and soon as I had sung
Methought she laid a grain upon my tongue.

XXXI

"Wherefore I sing, nor can from song refrain,
In honor of that blissful Maiden free,
Till from my tongue off-taken is the grain;
And after that thus said she unto me;
'My little Child, then will I come for thee
Soon as the grain from off thy tongue they take:
Be not dismayed, I will not thee forsake!' "

XXXII

This holy Monk, this Abbot—him mean I,
Touched then his tongue, and took away the grain;
And he gave up the ghost full peacefully;
And when the Abbot had this wonder seen,
His salt tears trickled down like showers of rain;
And on his face he dropped upon the ground,
And still he lay as if he had been bound.

XXXIII

Eke the whole Convent on the pavement lay,
Weeping and praising Jesu's Mother dear;
And after that they rose, and took their way,
And lifted up this Martyr from the bier,
And in a tomb of precious marble clear
Enclosed his uncorrupted body sweet.—
Where'er he be, God grant us him to meet!

XXXIV

Young Hew[1] of Lincoln! in like sort laid low
By cursèd Jews—thing well and widely known,
For it was done a little while ago—
Pray also thou for us, while here we tarry
Weak sinful folk, that God, with pitying eye,
In mercy would his mercy multiply
On us, for reverence of His Mother Mary!

The Jew's House in Lincoln

When said was all this miracle, each man
So sober was that wonder was to see,
Till that our Host to break the spell began
With jokes and chaff, first turning upon me
And speaking thus: "What man art thou?" quoth he.
"Thou seemest to be hunting for a hare,
For ever upon the ground I see thee stare.

"Draw near, I say, and look up merrily.
Beware now, sirs, and let this man have place.
He in the waist is shaped as well as I,
A chubby poppet for the arm's embrace

1. Hugh.

Of any woman small and fair of face.
Perchance the fairies claim him as their own,
For with a dreamy look he rides alone.

"But tell thy tale, as other folk have done,
A tale of mirth and that without delay."
"Mine Host," quoth I, "be not displeased with one
Who knoweth never a tale, save speak I may
A rhyme that long ago I learned to say."
"Yea, good," quoth he. "Some dainty thing it is
Methinketh by that roguish look of his."
[Then out of very mischief Chaucer made
A parody upon the rhymed romance,
A fashion of his day that was to fade
Before his own fresh poetry's advance.
He spoke it with his "elfish countenance"
Turned on the Host, whose ruddy visage wore
A puzzled look that deepened more and more.

'Twas of Sir Thopas, pink and white of mien,
A knight with saffron beard and seemly nose,
Who vowed his love unto the Fairy Queen
And would for her in mortal battle close
With a three-headed giant. Ere the foes
Had met, our champion his courage fed
With sugar, licorice, and gingerbread.]

"And then he clad his body in
Fine linen, white as was his skin,
  Trousers and also shirt;
And next his shirt a tunic sat,
A coat of mail went over that
  To keep his heart from hurt.

Chaucer

"His shield was all of gold so red,
And therein was a boar's grim head,
  A carbuncle beside;
And there he swore on ale and bread
That he would kill the giant dead
  Betide what might betide.

"His goodly steed he then bestrode,
And forth upon his way he rode
  Like sparkle from the fire.
Upon his crest he bore a tower
And, stuck therein, a lily flower.
  God save it from the mire!

"Because an errant knight was he,
He slept beneath the greenwood tree;
  A house would never do.
His helmet must his pillow be.
His charger "——

"No more of this, for Heaven's own dignity."
Broke in our Host. "In sooth, thou makest me
So weary with thy very silliness
That, so may God my soul and body bless,
Mine ears are aching from thy speech. Right, well
Thy story may be called rhyme doggerel.
The Devil take that tale of thine!" quoth he.

"Why so?" quoth I. "Why wilt thou hinder me
From rhyming more than any other man,
Since here I do the very best I can?"

Then roundly swore our Host as on we rode
And quoth: "Thy rhyming is not worth a toad.
All that thou dost is but to waste the time.
Sir, in one word, thou shalt no longer rhyme.
Plainly thou art no poet. But disclose
If thou can'st tell us anything in prose,
Something with mirth in it or moral lore."

"Gladly," quoth I, "if I may try once more,
I will you tell a little thing in prose
That ought to give you pleasure, I suppose,
Or else, in sooth, too critical you are.
It is a moral tale and known afar.
So hearken all to what I now will say,
And let me tell it to the end, I pray."

[Therewith the Poet, casting down his eyes
To hide the twinkle, with the April skies
Smiling above him, told the cavalcade
The longest, dullest story ever made,
The tale of Melibeus and his wife.
Her name was Prudence and she stilled all strife
With such sage counsels and grave preachments that
The story soothed the pilgrims, as they sat
Their drooping horses that soft afternoon,
To nodding slumber like a vesper tune.
Only the Host lent an attentive ear
From first to last, for he, so bold of cheer,
So ready from the Tabard Inn to roam,
Led but a sorry life of it at home.]

When ended was the tale, our Host began:
"By all the saints, as I'm a Christian man,
'Twould please me better than a cask of ale
If Goody Bailly might have heard this tale;
For she is no such gentle wife as had
This Melibeus. If I beat a lad,
One of my grooms or tapsters, she will bring
Great knobby staves, the heaviest she can swing,
And cry: 'Hit harder! slay 'em every one!

Beat 'em and break 'em! break 'em back and bone!'
Or if some neighbor or some friend of mine
Will not in church low to my wife incline,
Or seems in any way to grudge her grace,
When she comes home, she rampeth in my face
And crieth: 'Coward! go, avenge thy wife!
Now by the Mass, 'tis I will bear the knife,
And thou shalt have my distaff and go spin.'
From day to night she keepeth up the din.
'Alas!' she saith. 'That destiny should shape
My lot to wed a milksop and an ape,
A coward every man may put upon.
Thou can'st not guard the wife that thou hast won.'
This is my life, save I consent to fight,
Save out of doors I rush to do her right.
The only way to please her is to be
Like a wild lion, fierce and foolhardy.
I warrant some time she will make me slay
Some neighbor and then go the gallows way,
For I am dangerous with knife in hand,
Though truly against her I dare not stand,
For big she is in arms and passing strong,
As he shall find that doth her any wrong;
But from this subject let us pass away.

"My lord the Monk," quoth he, "be glad and gay.
It is your turn to tell a tale; hard by
Is Rochester, where we to-night shall lie.
Ride forth, my gracious lord, break not our game.
But by my troth I do not know your name,
Whether to call you my good lord Don John,
Or else Don Thomas, or Don Albion.

Of what house are ye by your father's kin?
Thou hast a comely color to thy skin;
A goodlier pasture thine than falls to most;
Thou art not like a penitent or ghost;
Thou hast some office of respect and ease;
Yea, faith, thou hast in charge the cellar keys.
By my father's soul and by my halidom,
Thou art a master when thou art at home,
No cloistered scholar and no chanting priest,
Lord of the larder art thou, at the least.''

This worthy Monk in patience took it all,
And said: "If now to me the turn doth fall,
I will do what I may to edify
This company with tales, and bye-and-bye,
On our return, perchance I will tell more,
For I am richly versed in saintly lore.
But tragedies at first shall make you merry;
I have a hundred in my monastery.
A tragedy, my hearers, is a story
Kept in old books, of one who. out of glory
And high prosperity and fair success
Hath fallen into utter wretchedness.
And that such tragedies should seem the worse,
'Tis usual to write them down in verse,
With long-drawn lines and with a sounding close;
But tragedies are also writ in prose,
And, too, in stanzas made in various wise.
This introduction should to you suffice.
Now hearken, if ye please, and hush your clatter,
But first, pray pardon me if in this matter
I should not in their order tell these things,

Be it of popes or emperors or kings,
After their ages, as in books we find,
But tell them some before and some behind,
Just as they chance to come into my mind;
I never was to study much inclined."

The Monk

[And so the Monk began with pompous air
To tell his tragedies, as counting there
An ebon rosary,—such dismal lore
The pilgrim faces lengthened more and more.
The Host could hardly brook another word,
But who should interrupt so great a lord?
Lucifer, Adam, Samson, Hercules,

Nebuchadnezzar and Belshazzar, these
He told about at first; then of a queen,
Zenobia, in golden fetters seen
To please the Roman mob; Pedro of Spain
Came next, by subtlety betrayed and slain;
Pedro of Cyprus; then the misery
Of him men called the Scourge of Lombardy;
The woe of Urgolino, starved to death;
How Nero yielded up his wicked breath;
How Holofernes died, Antiochus
And Alexander; then the treacherous
Slaying of Caesar; how on gallows shone
The bones of Croesus,—still the voice droned on:]

"So hanged on high was Croesus, the proud king;
His royal throne might him no whit avail.
Tragedy is no other sort of thing
Than this, which turneth singing into wail;
For Fortune ever will with strokes assail,
Taken at unawares, the glad and proud;
Yea, when men trust in her, then will she fail,
And cover her bright face as with a cloud."

"Ho!" quoth the Knight. "Good sir, no more, I plead.
What ye have said is quite enough, indeed;
More than enough; a little heaviness
Is quite enough for most mankind, I guess.
I say for mine own part it is distress,
When men have been in wealth and happiness,
To hear about their sudden fall, alas!
But joy it is to hear how poor men pass

Forth from their poverty and low estate,
And still climb up and still wax fortunate,
And so abide in safe prosperity.
Such thing is gladsome, as it seemeth me,
And of such thing 'twere sweet and good to tell."

"Yea," quoth our Host, "by Saint Paul's holy bell,
Ye say right sooth; this Monk, he prateth loud;
He told how 'Fortune covered with a cloud'
I wot not what, and talked of 'Tragedy'
As ye have heard, but faith! no remedy
It is for us to wail or to complain
Of what is done, and, also, 'tis a pain,
As ye have said, to hear of heaviness.
Sir Monk, no more of this, so God you bless!
Your tale annoyeth all this company;
Such talking is not worth a butterfly,
For in it there's not any sport nor game.
Wherefore, Sir Monk, Don Peter by your name,
I do beseech you, from your abbey cells
Bring lighter lore, for wer't not for the bells
That clink upon your bridle as ye ride,
By the King of Heaven, Who for us sinners died,
I should ere this have fallen down for sleep,
Although the mud and mire were ne'er so deep.
Then had your story all been told in vain,
For bootless 'twere that preacher should explain
His text without an audience, and I
Am he you most are bound to edify,
For I am judge what tale of all shall win
The promised supper at the Tabard Inn.
Sir, tell a tale of hunting." "Nay, not I.

I have no mind to idle vanity,"
Answered the Monk. "My part is done, go on."

Then to the Prioresses priest, Sir John,
Called out our Host, with careless speech and free:
"Come here, Sir Priest! ride in the midst with me!
Tell us a story that shall make us glad.
Be blithe as if thy beast were not so bad.
What though it be an ugly nag and lean!
If he will serve thee, care thou not a bean.
Look that thine heart be merry evermore."

"Yes, sir," quoth he; "yes, Host. As ye implore,
I will be merry, I will make you fun."
And right anon his tale he hath begun,
And thus he said unto us every one,
This pleasant Priest, this goodly man, Sir John:—

TALE OF SIR JOHN, THE PRIEST

Once a poor widow, who the burden felt
Of her increasing years, all humbly dwelt
In a small cottage, standing in a dale
Beside a grove. This subject of my tale,
Since the last day that saw her still a wife,
In patience led a spare and simple life,
For scant her store. By thrifty management
Of such as God in pity to her sent
She kept herself and daughters twain. Three sows
Of goodly size she had, as many cows,
And one sheep, Moll. Two rooms sufficed for all,
And smutty was her bower and eke her hall,

In which full many a slender meal she ate.
There passed her throat no morsel delicate;

The Nun's Priest

No pungent sauces needed she to whet
Her appetite; she ate what she could get,
And over-eating never made her ill.
Her physic was low diet, work, a will
Submissive to her lot. 'Twas not the gout
Kept her from dancing when the pipes were out,
Nor did the apoplexy cloud her head,
For wine she drank not, neither white nor red.
Her board was set mostly with white and black,
Milk and brown bread, in which she found no
lack,

Broiled bacon, or an egg, her fare to vary,
When trade was thriving in her modest dairy.

A poultry yard she had, fenced all about
With close-set sticks, and a dry ditch without.
Herein she kept a cock, called Chanticleer.
Not all the land for crowing had his peer.
His voice rang merrier than the organ plays
At mass within the church on holidays.
His crowing on his roost marked off the time
More surely than a clock or abbey chime.
By instinct, not by mathematic lore,
He knew each hour of all the twenty-four,
And best the hour before the dawn, when he
So crew, his crow might not amended be.
His comb, more red than coral fine, was all
Indented like a battlemented wall.
His bill was black, and as the jet it shone;
Like azure were the legs he strutted on;
Nails white as lilies when the buds unfold,
And all his body shone like burnished gold.
This gentle cock to serve his every whim
Had seven hens, all wondrous like to him
In color, and the one with fairest throat
Was called the lovely lady Pertelote.
Courteous she was, discreet and debonair,
Companionable, and herself she bare
So prudently, since she was seven-night old
She had the heart of Chanticleer in hold,
Locked hard and fast, like prisoner in cell.
He loved her so that with him all was well.
And such a joy it was to hear them sing,

When up the sky the sun began to spring,
In sweet accord: "My Love is gone away."
For at that time, as I have oft heard say,
The beasts and birds knew how to speak and sing.
And so befell, when dawn was whitening,
As Chanticleer, amid his household all,
Sat on a beam, there in the widow's hall,
And next to him this beauteous Pertelote,
This Chanticleer began to groan in throat
As man that in his dream is troubled sore.
And when Dame Pertelote thus heard him snore,
She was aghast and said: "O fie, my dear!
What aileth you that such strange sounds I hear?
A pretty sleeper you! For shame!" And he
Replied to her and said with dignity:
"Your pardon, Madame. Take it not amiss.
A dreadful dream I dreamed; because of this,
Mine heart is even yet in sore affright.
Now God forbid it bode some evil plight!
God keep me safe! For I would have you know
I in my dream was roaming to and fro
Within our yard, when I beheld a beast
Like to a hound, who would have made his feast
Upon my body,—would have had me dead.
His color betwixt a yellow and a red,
Save that his tail and ears were tipped with black;
His snout, that followed keen upon my track,
Was small; his eyes so glowing-fierce that I
Still of his look for terror almost die.
This caused the groans which gave you such a start."

"Avaunt!" quoth she. "Fie on you, chicken-heart!
Alas!" quoth she, "for, by that God above,
Now have ye lost mine heart and all my love;
I cannot love a coward, by my faith,
For certes, whatso any woman saith,
We all desire, if so it might befall,
To have brave husbands, wise and liberal,
Not fools nor niggards, nay, nor one whose knees
Begin to shake when he a weapon sees,
Nor any braggart, by that God above!
How durst ye say for shame unto your Love
That anything might make your soul afeared?
Have ye no manly heart and have a beard?
Alas! and can ye be dismayed by dreams?
Nothing, God wot, but vanity there seems
To be in them, induced by overeating,
Unwholesome gases in the stomach meeting,
Or temperament, determined by the blood.
Your dream may easily be understood
As born from an excess of humor red
Which causeth folk to dream of arrows sped
Against them, fire that shoots a crimson light,
Great beasts with gaping jaws eager to bite,
Of strife and snapping pups, both large and small,—
Red dreams engendered of red humor all;
Just as black humor dyes our dreaming wholly
With its own hue of dismal melancholy,
And sleeping men cry out black bulls and bears
Are on them, or black devil at them tears.
Of other humors could I tell, that make
Full many a sleeper on his pallet quake,
But I will pass as lightly as I can.

"Lo, Cato, who was such a learnèd man,
Said he not thus: 'Make no account of dreams'?
Now, sir," quoth she, "when down from off the beams
We fly, for God's love take some laxative.
So may my soul be saved, so may I live,
As this my counsel ye may surely trust.
Of humor red and humor black ye must
Go purge yourself. Though no apothecary
Is in this town, I have an eye so wary
I can myself point out to you the herbs
That best will rid you of whate'er disturbs;
And in our very yard those herbs I'll find
Which are by nature specially designed
To cause a nausea and the stomach clear.
Forget not this, as God doth hold us dear!
Ye are inclined unto the humor red;
Take heed that when the sun is overhead
Ye do not heat your blood too much, for so
Fever or ague soon will lay you low.
A day or two, for your digestion's sake,
Ye shall eat worms, ere ye begin to take
Your laxative of laurel, hellebore,
Of dogwood berries, centaury and more,
Spurge, fumitory, ivy growing waste
Here in our yard and pleasant to the taste.
Pick 'em up right as they grow and eat 'em down.
Be merry! for your race's high renown,
Dread ye no dream. Now can I say no more."

"Madame," quoth he, "gramercy[1] for your lore,
But as for this Don Cato, ay, the same
That hath for wisdom such prodigious fame,

[1] Thanks.

Though he to dreams would have us pay no heed,
By Heaven, men may in ancient volumes read
Of many a man of more authority
Than ever Cato was, or may I die,
Who holds the very contrary and knows
From true experience that dreams disclose
The coming joy or sorrow, peace or strife,
That wait on mortals in this present life.
There is no need of formal argument;
The facts themselves a perfect proof present.
One of the greatest authors that men know,
The Roman orator, Don Cicero,
Tells how, once on a time, two comrades went
Upon a pilgrimage, with good intent,
And needs must some unkindly chance them bring
Unto a city where large gathering
Of folk had filled the few small inns and shut
Each door against them; no, not even a hut
They found, in which the two of them might lie.
And so perforce they parted company
For that one night, each going his own way
To seek a nook where he might rest till day.
The one, at the bottom of an inn yard lay
In oxen-stall, upon a heap of hay;
His mate found lodging at another inn,
So did his enterprise or fortune win
The better bed, as human chances fall.
But long before the dawn-light touched the wall,
He dreamt he heard his fellow on him call
And say: 'Alas! for in an oxen-stall
This night I shall be murdered where I lie.
Now help me, brother dear, or else I die;

In utmost haste come thou to me,' he cried.
The sleeper started up, all terrified,
But once awake, he turned him on his side,
Nor thought what might that dream of his betide,
For he held dreams to be but vanity.
Thus twice within his sleeping dreamèd he,
And at the third time did the vision feign
His friend before him, saying: 'I am slain.
Behold my bloody wounds, how deep and wide!
Arise up early in the morning-tide,
And at the west gate of the town,' quoth he,
'A cart piled high with dung there shalt thou see,
In which my body secretly is hid.
Do thou that cart arrest and those who did
This cruel murder on me for my gold.'
And every point of that foul crime he told
With a full piteous face, all pale of hue.
And be assured he found his dream full true;
For on the morrow, soon as it was day,
Unto his fellow's inn he took his way,
And when he came unto this oxen-stall
Upon his fellow he began to call.
The keeper of the inn replied anon
And said to him: 'Your fellow, sir, is gone.
At daybreak from the city he departed.'
Then waxed the pilgrim somewhat anxious-hearted,
Remembering the dream that he had dreamt;
And forth he hastened, on his errand bent,
To the west gate, and there saw passing out,
As to manure the fields, a dung-cart stout,
In all respects like that whose use and plan
Ye heard recounted by the murdered man.

And he with hardy heart began to cry
For law and justice on this felony.
'My fellow murdered is this night,' he said,
'And in this cart he lieth stiff and dead.
I lift my voice against the magistrates
That ought to safeguard all within these gates.
Help, help! alas! here lies my fellow slain!'
What needeth more to make the story plain?
The people rushed and cast the cart to ground
And in the middle of the dung they found
The murdered man, whose wounds were wet and new.

"O blissful God, that art so good and true,
Behold, the slayer thou wilt surely slay.
Murder will out; that see we day by day.
Murder so loathsome is and horrible
To God, whose justice doeth all things well,
He will not let it undiscovered be,
Though it lie hid a year, or two, or three.
Murder will out; this is the certain end.
And right anon that town's officials send
And take that inn-keeper and carter both
And rack them till their wicked mouths, though loth,
Confess the crime. The rest is shortly said.
They hanged them by the neck till they were dead.

"This shows that dreams are to be held in dread,
And certes, in the same old book I read,
Right in the very chapter after this,—
I am no liar, by my hope of bliss—
How once two men, that would have crossed the sea
For certain reasons, found the wind to be

Against them and were therefore forced to wait
Within a city that was situate
Full pleasantly upon a haven-side.
At last one day, about the eventide,
The wind began to change and blow them fair.
Blithely did they unto their rest repair
And planned to sail full early, but there fell
To one of them a very miracle,
For as he sleeping on his pallet lay,
He dreamed a wondrous dream at break of day.

There seemed a man beside his bed to stand
And bid him tarry longer on the land,
Speaking these words: 'If thou to-morrow wend,
Thou shalt be drowned; my tale is at an end.'
He woke and told his fellow what he dreamt,
And prayed him to abandon his intent,
And for at least another day to wait.
With mockery replied his faring-mate,
Who slept beside him, laughing him to scorn.
'Not by a dream,' quoth he, 'is overborne
My purpose to push forward my affairs.
I prize not at a straw thy sleeping scares;
For dreams are vanities, mere jests of slumber;
Men dream of owls and monkeys without number
And many a foolery. In dreams men see
Such things as never were nor yet shall be.
But since 'tis plain that thou wilt here abide,
And let thy chance go by and lose the tide,
God knows I grieve for it; and so good-day.'
And thus he took his leave and went his way.
But ere the ship one half her course had sailed—

I know not why, nor what mischance it ailed—
By some ill-hap her keel was rent asunder,
And that good ship and all on board went under
In sight of other vessels close beside
That sailed out with them on the selfsame tide.
And therefore, lovely Pertelote, my dear,
By ancient instances I've made it clear
That no man carelessly should disregard
A dream, for I assure thee, on my word,
Full many a dream demands most careful heed.

"Lo, in the life of Saint Kenelm I read—
The son of Kenulph, he who ruled supreme
In Mercia—how Kenelm once dreamt a dream;
A little ere his murder came to pass
He saw it in a dream as in a glass.
His nurse explained his vision every whit
And bade the royal child, because of it,
Beware of treason; yet, but seven year old,
So holy was his heart it might not hold
Such warning nor the dread of secret hurt.
By Heaven above, but I would give my shirt
If ye had read his legend, as have I.
Dame Pertelote, I say, and do not lie,
Macrobius, that writ, as all men know,
The vision of the worthy Scipio,
Affirmeth dreams, declaring them to be
Warnings of things that men shall after see.
And furthermore, I pray you, study well
The Scriptures, in the book of Daniel,
To find if he held dreams a vanity.
Read, too, of Joseph, and then shall ye see

Whether or no some dreams (I say not all)
Forebode events that afterward befall.
The king of Egypt, too, Don Pharaoh,
His baker and his butler, let us know
If they found dreams had power to overwhelm.
Who reads the chronicles of any realm
May learn of dreams full many a wondrous thing.

"Lo, Croesus, who of Lydia was king,
Did he not dream he sat upon a tree,
Which signified that hangèd he should be?
Lo, here, Andromache, brave Hector's wife,
The day that Hector was to lose his life,
She dreamt upon the very night before
How he should perish and her heart be sore,
If on that day he donned his battle-mail.
She warned him, but her words might not avail.
He went into the fight nor came again,
For there by fierce Achilles was he slain.
But 'twere too long to tell that fatal sally.
Besides, it is nigh day, I may not dally.
Shortly I say it is my firm decision
That I must look to have, upon this vision,
Adversity; and I say furthermore
That by your laxatives I set no store,
For they are poisons,—bitter, too, as gall,
And I defy 'em, love 'em not at all.

"Now let us speak of mirth and leave all this.
Dame Pertelote, so may I come to bliss,
As God has granted me one ample grace,
For when I see the beauty of your face,

Ye are so scarlet-red about your eyes
That all my trouble in contentment dies.
For just as sure as *In principio*
Mulier est hominis confusio—
Madame, the meaning of this Latin is
Woman's her husband's joy and all his bliss[1]—
I am so full of solace and delight
That I defy the visions of the night."
And with that word he flew down from the rafter,
For it was morning, and his hens flew after;
And with a "chuck" he called them out of door,
Where he had found a grain of corn. No more
Afraid, he strutted grand and lion-grim
Upon his toes, as 'twould dishonor him
To set his lordly foot upon the ground.
He chucked, whenever he a kernel found,
And all his hens came running to his call.
Thus royal, as a monarch in his hall,
Leave I this Chanticleer, and haste to tell
The adventure that in after time befell.

When that spring month in which the world began,
The month of March, when God created man,
Had passed, and April's thirty days were gone,
Upon the third of May the doom came on.
Befell that Chanticleer, in all his pride,
His seven wives out walking by his side,
Cast up his eyes unto the shining sun
That on its heavenly path so far had run
This cock by nature knew that it was prime
Of day, and crowed a welcome to the time.
With blissful voice he crowed and shrill and high.

1 How about the cock's translation?

"The sun," he said, "is clomb up in the sky
Forty degrees and more, well wot I this.
O Madame Pertelote, my worldly bliss,
Hark to these blissful birds how sweet they sing,
And see the flowers how fresh and fair they spring.
Full is mine heart of solace and of revel."
But suddenly there fell on him great evil,
For ever the latter end of joy is woe.
God knows that worldly joy is swift to go,
And were an author skilled in words he might
Safely within a chronicle it write
As sovereign fact of human destiny.
Now hearken, all ye wise. I testify
That though my story common faith might shake,
'Tis just as true as *Launcelot of the Lake*,
That old romance which women all believe.
So here I turn again my tale to weave.

A crafty fox, beyond all foxes sly,
That now three years within the grove hard by
Made his abode, this very night, by clue
Of high imagination, had burst through
The widow's fence of twigs into the yard
Where Chanticleer was wont to walk in guard
Of his fair wives, and noiselessly had sped
To the safe shelter of a cabbage bed.
There till the noon he lurked with pricked-up ear,
Biding his time to fall on Chanticleer,
As is the wont of these assassins when
They lie in wait to murder guileless men.
O new Iscariot! O Ganelon,
That wert the death of Roland! O Sinon,

The Chair of St. Augustine, Canterbury Cathedral

False Greek that madest Troy a waste forlorn!
O Chanticleer, accursèd be the morn
When thou didst fly from off the cottage beams
Into the yard, forgetful of thy dreams
That showed thee, as a shadow in a glass,
Calamity. But that must come to pass
Which was predestined, so some scholars say;
But any perfect scholar knows that they
Who lecture on theology dispute
This matter and each other's views confute,

A hundred thousand talkers not agreed.
Not I can sift the question out, indeed,
As can the holy doctor Augustine,
Boethius the sage, or Bradwardine,
Professor and archbishop both in one.
Whether by will of God my deeds are done,
Or by my own, is more than I can say;
Or if my will is free but to obey
Eternal knowledge and divine decree.
These heavenly matters are too hard for me;
At secret doors 'tis not for me to knock;
I only tell the story of a cock,
That, to his sorrow,—when he should have kept
The warning of his dream in mind, nor stept
Abroad so lightly,—took his wife's advice,
Though not her medicines; so Paradise
Was lost through woman's counsel which to woe
Brought all the race in making Adam go
From Eden where, full merry and at ease,
He lived his life beneath the garden trees.
But since my eye among the pilgrims sees
Some I would be unwilling to displease
By bringing woman's counsel into blame,
Pray pass it by, as said in sport and game.
Read authors on this theme and see what they
Of woman and her counsels have to say.
These are the cock's opinions; not my own;
No harm have I of any woman known.

Deep in the sand, to bathe her merrily,
Lies Pertelote, and all her sisters by,
Basking in sun; and Chanticleer so free

Sang merrier than the mermaid in the sea—
For in an ancient Latin book 'tis told
How sweet the Sirens sing on sands of gold—
And so befell that, as he cast his eye
Where o'er the cabbage bed a butterfly
Went wandering, he saw the fox crouched low.
No spirit then was left in him to crow,
But sharp he cried "cok, cok" and started back
As man whom sudden enemies attack;
For thus instinctively a beast doth know
And seek to flee from its appointed foe,
Though ne'er before it have the creature eyed.

This Chanticleer, when he the fox espied,
Would fain have fled, but spake Don Russell low
And soft: "Fair sir, alas! where would ye go?
Be not afraid of me that am your friend,
For I were worse than devil would I rend
Those splendid plumes or cause you any ill.
I am not come such mischief to fulfill.
My cause of coming, to confess the thing,
Was but to hear you lift your voice and sing;
For verily ye have as blithe a tone
As any Angel chanting by the Throne,
And have more skill and sympathy in song
Than did to famous bard or sage belong.
My lord your father—God his sweet soul bless!—
And, too, your mother, of her gentleness,
Have been within my house, to my great pleasure;
And, certès, sir, your friendship would I treasure.
But as for song, I tell you, as I prize
The precious seeing of my own two eyes,

I never heard such singing, save your own,
As when your father raised his clarion tone
To greet the dawn. From heart that cock would sing
And, so to make his voice the farther ring,
He put such effort forth that both his eyes
Would wink, the while his crowing pierced the skies;
And standing on his tiptoes therewithal,
His neck he would outstretch most long and small.
He was, too, for discretion so renowned
That not a soul in all the region round
For wisdom nor for song might him surpass.
True, in the book of *Don Burnel the Ass*
I've read about that very clever cock
Who, in resentment of uncivil knock
A scholar in rash childhood gave him, bode
His time, and when the Church would have bestowed
A benefice on his tormentor, crowed
So late, the tardy riser, though he rode
Unpriestly fast, arrived at church too late
And missed his fortune; but I would not rate
The cunning of his craft one moment by
Your father's prudence and sagacity.
But now, for sweet Saint Charity, I pray
That you to me your gift of song display.
Can you with your great father's strains compete?"
This Chanticleer his wings began to beat,
Nor could the treason of the fox espy,
So was he ravished with his flattery.

Alas, ye lords! within your courts are heard
Full many a flattering tongue and glozing word
That please your lordships better, by my faith,

Than what plain Honesty unto you saith.
Go read *Ecclesiasticus* and see
What treason lurks in soft-voiced flattery.

This Chanticleer stood high upon his toes,
Stretching his shining neck; then did he close
His eyes and raised aloft a ringing note.
Up sprang the fox and caught him by the throat,
And on his back fast bore him toward the wood,
For yet he was not sighted nor pursued,
This robber who the widow's yard had raided.
O Destiny, that may not be evaded!
Alas, that Chanticleer e'er left the beams!
Alas, that Pertelote made light of dreams!
And on a Friday all this trouble fell.
O Venus, Chanticleer had served thee well;
His seven wives devoutly did he cherish;
Why would'st thou let him on thy Friday perish?
O poet Geoffrey,[1] master sovereign,
That mournedst Richard Coeur de Lion, slain
Upon a Friday, would I had thy lore
To rail on Friday and her deeds deplore!
Then would I lift a long, lamenting strain
For Chanticleer, his peril and his pain.

Certes, such outcry and bewailing sore
Was ne'er by lovely ladies made before,—
Not e'en when Troy crashed down and Pyrrhus took
King Priam by the beard and fiercely shook
His naked sword above that milk-white head
And smote him so—as made those hens for dread
Of murder to their lord, but shrillest rose

[1] Not Geoffrey Chaucer, but Geoffrey of Vinesauf.

The shrieks of Pertelote, louder than those
That tore the bosom of the Carthage queen
When Hasdrubal her husband slain was seen,
With all his town in flames for funeral pyre;
Then waxed that queen for anguish and for ire
So desperate she plunged into the blaze
And sealed with constancy her regal days.
O woeful hens, your wail—alas, for pity!—
Was such as rose, when Nero burned the city
Of Rome, from senators' distracted wives,
Who saw their hapless lords yield up their lives;
And for this guiltless grief those dames were slain
By wicked Nero. Now my tale again!

This simple widow and her daughters twain
Heard the hens' cries and started forth amain
And, rushing from the cottage door, what should
They see but, making swiftly for the wood,
The fox, upon whose back their rooster lay!
They cried: "Help, help! alack! and weyleway!
The fox!" and into wild pursuit they broke,
And, too, with staves came all the neighbor folk;
Ran Colle our dog, and Talbot, and Gerlànd,
And Malkin, with a distaff in her hand;
Ran cow and calf, and e'en the very hogs,
So were they scared for barking of the dogs,
Shouting of men and brandished pole and stake;
They ran as if their panting hearts would break;
They squealed like fiends in hell whom torments vex;
Cackled the ducks as men would wring their necks;
The geese for fright flew up above the trees;
Out of the hive there came the swarm of bees;

So hideous was the noise that, bless my soul!
Jack Straw and all his rabble did not roll
One half the clamor through our London town
When they would put the Flemish merchants down.
As bellowed up that day behind the fox,
For they had trumpets made of brass, and box,
Of horn, of bone, in which they blew and sounded,
And shrieked and whooped withal till heaven, con-
  founded
By such an uproar, seemed about to fall.

Now, fellow-pilgrims, hearken one and all.
Lo, fickle Fortune! how she overthrows
All suddenly the triumph of her foes!
This cock, that lay upon the fox's back,
For all his terror said: "Upon your track
They cry so loud, I should, sir, in your place—
God help me!—call to them: 'Ye well may face
Toward home again, ye bawling rustics all!
The very pestilence upon you fall!
Now am I on the borders of the wood
Where, in despite of you, the cock my food
Shall be, for right anon his blood I'll spill.' "

Answered the fox: "In faith, and so I will."
And as he spoke that word, loosing the vice
Of his sharp jaws, the rooster in a trice
Broke from his mouth and flew into a tree.
And when the fox perceived the trick, quoth he:

"Alas, O Chanticleer! I have with you
Been too abrupt; apologies are due;

I frightened you by my rough-seeming way
When from your yard I carried you away.
But, sir, there was no wrong in mine intent.
Come down and let me tell you what I meant.
I'll speak the truth to you, upon mine oath."

"Nay, then," quoth Chanticleer, "beshrew us both,
But first beshrew myself, both bones and skin,
If more than once thy falsehoods take me in.
I'll sing for thee no more, nor need'st thou think
Thy flatteries again shall make me wink,
For he that winketh when he ought to see,
Heaven send him grief! This lore I owe to thee.'

"Nay," quoth the fox, "a better prayer is this—
My thanks—may his best plans go all amiss
Who chatters when he ought to hold his tongue."

And so you see, my hearers old and young,
What comes of trusting flatterers. And all
Who count this but a tale nonsensical
About a fox, a rooster, and a hen,
May yet a moral draw from it for men;
For Saint Paul saith that all that hath been writ
Is writ for our instruction. Ponder it;
Garner the grain and let the chaff blow by.

Now, gracious God, shed on us from on high
Thy holy blessing, keep our lives from vice,
And bring us all at last to Paradise.

Rochester Castle and Grounds

[The Host and all the pilgrims praised the tale,
But now the flow of talk began to fail,
For they had jaunted fifteen miles that day
And heard some seven stories. Well we may
Believe the sunset light found every face
The gladder for the near-by halting-place,
And plume and sleeve and mantle were set trim,
And, as they might, they trolled a Latin hymn
In riding, like the worthy folk they were,
Through castled and cathedraled Rochester.]

The Tomb of Geoffrey Chaucer, Westminster Abbey

THE THIRD DAY

[Had Death but waited till the Master's hand
Had bodied out the book so richly planned,
Then would we know, as now we but divine,
How tale with tale, and jest with jest combine.
Methinks that Chaucer laugheth in his sleeve
To see the rows of painful scholars weave
Their russet learning through his shining web
Of fun and fancy, but their task is sped
So well we may with some assurance group
These third-day stories of the pilgrim troop.

With jocund hearts they rose from blissful sleep
Under the shadow of the Norman keep

Which guards the pleasant city now as then,
Knelt in the stately church, as Christian men
Behooves, and gazed so long about the shops
That fell the oaths like summer water-drops
From Harry Bailly, till, at last arrayed,
Went clattering forth his motley cavalcade.
First rode the Knight and Squire, with Yeoman by,
And next to these, who ranked in chivalry
Above the rest, came those in special grace
Of Holy Church, the Monk of rosy face,
And Prioress, with her nun and priest close after,—
Stalwart Sir John, whose eyes still twinkled laughter.
The Franklin and the Lawyer, cheek by jowl,
Cantered behind, and then that thrifty soul,
The Doctor, in his glowing robes; with these
The Merchant strove to bear himself at ease.
Apart there jogged, with sweet, abstracted look,
The Clerk of Oxford, and our Poet took,
I ween, place by him, while the Parson grave
Held with his Ploughman brother—God him save
For saintly heart beneath the rustic smock!
The five spruce craftsmen followed in a flock.
The rabble of the train brought up the rear
With bagpipes, song, and shout—such noisy cheer
Our Host, who would not have the gentles vexed,
Yet loved the revelry, was oft perplexed
To hold an even rule,—so swift to wrath
The Miller was, so loud the Wife of Bath
In spicy speech, the Manciple so sly,
The Cook so prompt the roadside ale to try,
The Sailor stormy-rough and, worst of all,
Those three who claimed the world from sin to call,

The Friar with his roundelays, the base,
Foul-spoken Summoner, whose flaring face
Frighted the children in the way, and he
Whose yellow locks streamed loose for jollity,
The Pardoner; while hindmost of them all
The jealous Steward watched. On whom to call

The Doctor of Physic

For the first tale? Certes, a man of lore,
The Doctor, who the Host's heart made so sore
With telling of the little Roman maid,
Virginia, slain by her father's blade,
As love's best gift in bitter times, that he
For very pity swore most lustily.]

"Alas! but truly, O my master dear,
This is a grievous thing for men to hear;
But pass it by. God save thee, hair and hide,
And all the organs that thou hast inside,
And all thy physic bottles, all thy plasters
And ointment jars. God keep 'em from disasters!
Bless thee and all thy drugs our Mother Mary,
For thou art like a very dignitary
Of Holy Church. Thou art a man of fame,
As I judge men, by Saint Ron—what's-his-name.
Said I not well? No scholar-tongue is mine,
But what I know, I know,—and this, in fine,
That I have caught such heartache from thy tale,
That treacle, or a draught of corny ale,
Or laughter-moving story, it will cost
To cure me of it, else my heart is lost
For pity of this innocent young maid.
Thou rascal here, thou Pardoner," he said,
"Tell us some mirthful thing, all jest and game."

Alehouse with Alestake

"Yea," quoth he, "by your Saint Ron—what's-his-name.
But first here at this tavern let me take
A toss of ale and bit of breakfast-cake."

The gentles right anon began to cry:
"Nay, let him tell us no indecency.

Tell us some sober story that affords
A moral. Then we'll gladly hear his words."

"Agreed," quoth he, "but give me time to think
Of something virtuous, the while I drink.

"My lords," quoth he, "in churches when I preach,
Much pains I take for a sonorous speech,
And ring it out as roundly as a bell,
For I have learned by rote all that I tell.
My text is still the same and ever was:
Radix malorum est Cupiditas."[1]

[Then shamelessly he told his tricks of trade,—
How he pretended that his pardons made
Folk clean of sin,—that guilt might purchase
    grace
By touch of rubbish in his relic-case;
How charms he had,—a mitten which, should one
But, for a price, his hand within it run,
Would give him luck in sowing wheat and pease;
And charms to save the cattle from disease,
As holy shoulder-bone of Jewish sheep,
That, dipped into a spring, would surely keep
All creatures sound that drank thereof; yet
    through
His false there ran a hidden vein of true.]

"If that the husbandman from his repose
Rise every morning ere the rooster crows
And taste this well, nor from that custom cease,
His farm shall prosper and his stock increase."

[1] The love of money is the root of all evil.

The jeering scoundrel then went on to say
That his best trick to make the rustics pay
Their hard-won groats into his greedy hand
Was this,—he told them they might understand
That those who did not to the altar hie
To view his relics and his pardons buy,
Dared not because they had such frightful sin
Upon their souls,—and then the coins rained in.]

"And so by frauds and fooleries I clear
Full easily a hundred marks a year.
I mount the pulpit, pull a solemn face,
And when the silly people are in place,
I preach this that I told you just before,
And add a hundred lies and juggles more.
Then lean I forward, stretching out my neck,
And east and west upon the people beck
And bow like pigeon on a barn. My tongue
Wags fast, and all about my hands are flung,
So that to see my gains is very bliss;
And ever preach I against avarice.
The end of all my preaching is to make
Folk give me money; for no other sake
Than this I plead with them, their pence to win,
And nowise for correction of their sin;
For when their bodies to their graves are brought,
Their souls may go blackberrying, for aught
I care. 'Tis thus full many a sermon's made,
Not in the way of godliness, but trade,
To tickle gentlefolk by flattery
And win advancement through hypocrisy;
Or for vainglory, or for hate, for when

I dare not openly fall out with men
To whom I bear a grudge, I can them sting
With bitter tongue in course of sermoning,
So that if any one hath done despite
To me or to my brethren, there shall light
A scandal on him and a lasting shame,
For though, in sooth, I do not speak his name,
By signs and otherwise I make him known;
So he who seeks our harm secures his own.
Thus under hue of holiness I spit
My venom out and take my joy of it.

"The purpose of my preaching is but this,
To cure my audience of avarice;
Therefore my theme is yet and ever was,
Radix malorum est Cupiditas.
Thus do I preach, and for a goodly price,
Against what is my own especial vice;
Yet though myself am guilty of that sin,
To reformation other folk I win,
And by my words I cause them to repent;
But that is not my principal intent,—
I preach for money, nothing more nor less,
Because it lets me live in laziness.

"To spice my preaching, I would have you know,
I tell old tales of deeds done long ago,
For simple folk love songs and stories old;
Such things in memory they well can hold.
And thus I thrive, for while by sermoning
The gold and silver to my purse I bring,
Trow ye that I would take the foolish vow

Of voluntary poverty? Not now,
Nor ever; I will roam through sundry lands
To preach and beg, nor labor with my hands.
I have no shame in beggary, not I;
Nor would I baskets make and live thereby,
Like the Apostles. Nay, but I will eat
The finest of the cheese and of the wheat.
The poorest lad shall give a groat to me,
The poorest widow wool, although she see
Her children—what care I?—for hunger pine.
Nay, I will drink the liquor of the vine,
And many a roistering night in revel spend.
But hearken, gentles! hear me to the end.

"Your liking 'tis that I shall tell a tale.
Now I have drunk my draught of corny ale,
So virtuous a story I recall,
It should, in reason, please your worships all;
For though I be myself a vicious man,
A moral tale to you recite I can,—
One that I use in preaching on the sin
Of avarice. Be still and I'll begin."

THE PARDONER'S TALE

In Flanders once there dwelt a company
Of wild young men, who in debauchery
And folly lived, in all intemperance;
With harps and lutes and citterns would they dance
Both day and night, and eat around the table
In superfluity abominable,
And drink until the wine, stronger than they,

The Pardoner

Threw them upon the floor; so day by day
With gluttony and drunkenness and dice
They made unto the Devil sacrifice
In his own church, I mean the tavern, where
It grisly was to hear how they would swear,
And each would laugh to see his fellow sin.
[Then must the Pardoner from habit spin
A sermon on the wickedness of drink
And shame of gluttony, with many a wink
Directed to his cronies in the train.]
O gluttony, it is the body's bane!
Alas! alas! that for a throat so short
Is east and west and north and south resort
For dainties that, with labor and with slaughter,
Must men procure from earth and air and water!

What trouble is it delicates to find!
These cooks, how they must pound and strain and
grind,
And change, to please thy palate, by their spices
Of leaf and bark and root, and all devices,
The taste of things, till sauces new invite
As to new meats the whetted appetite.
Alas! and from the bones knock out must they
The marrow, for they cast no thing away
That may go through the gullet, soft and sweet;
But dead in soul is he who lives to eat.
[And even thus rebuked he drunken men,
That through the nose say "Samson, Samson"; then
Dicers and gamblers chid he even thus,
And then blasphemers, with a mischievous
Sign toward the Host; then, lest all patience fail,
At last the Pardoner took up his tale.]

These three chief revelers, of whom I tell,
Before the ringing of the matin bell
Had set them in a tavern down to drink;
And as they sat they heard a hand-bell clink
Before a corpse that journeyed to his grave.
Then called one to his boy, a clever knave:
"Be off," quoth he, "as fast as thou can'st hie,
And ask what corpse is this that passeth by,
And look the name in no wise be forgot."

"Sir," quoth this boy, "forsooth it needeth not.
I heard it told two hours before ye came;
Of one of your old fellows 'tis the name;
And suddenly the man was slain to-night,

As, drunk, he sat upon his bench upright;
There came a stealthy thief, whom men call
Death,
That in this country steals the people's breath.
And with his spear he smote his heart in twain,
And went his way. A thousand hath he slain
Since fell the pestilence upon the land.
And, master, in his presence should ye stand,
Methinks 'twere well ye should of him beware;
So sly an adversary needeth care;
Look lest he lie in wait at every door.
My mother told me this; I say no more."

Quoth the innkeeper, who was standing near:
"The child saith sooth, for he hath slain this
year,
And not a mile away, within a town,
Men, women, children, servants, up and down.
I trow his home is there, by sweet Saint Mary!
Great wisdom were it that a man be wary,
Lest Death do him dishonor. Ware ye, sir!"

"Ha, by the Mass!" replied this reveler.
"Is it such peril with that foe to meet?
I'll seek him both by footpath and by street,
And that I swear. I fear him not a feather.
Hearken, my fellows! we are three together.
Let each of us give hand unto the other,
And each become as brother unto brother,
And we will slay this wicked traitor, Death.
This robber, that so many murdereth,
He shall himself be slain, ere it be night."

Together have these three their promise plight
To live and die each one of them with other
As if he were in sooth his own born brother;
And up they start in drunken rage and go
Forth to that town of which, but just ago,
The innkeeper had told them. On the way
Full many a grisly oath they swear, and say,—
Because the wine has made their courage stout,—
Death shall be dead, if they may find him out.

When they had gone not fully half a mile,
Right as they would have trodden o'er a stile,
A poor old man they met. In humble wise
All courteous, with dim and downcast eyes,
He so saluted them: "Lords, God you såve!"
Of these three revelers the proudest gave
Rude answer: "What, old churl of sorry grace,
Why art thou muffled so, all save thy face?
Why livest thou so long, to go a-crook?"

Full in his face that agèd man did look
And answered thus: "Because I cannot find
A man, though I should leave this land behind
And wend to India, and search, in sooth,
All towns and villages, will change his youth
For my old age; so must I keep it still
As long a time as it may be God's will.
Not even Death, alas! my life will have.
Thus do I walk, as restless for my grave,
And on the ground, which is my mother's gate,
Go knocking with my staff early and late,
And saying: 'Dear my mother, let me in!

Lo, how I vanish, flesh and blood and skin!
Alas! when shall my bones come to their rest?
Mother, with you I'd change the treasure-chest
Within my chamber, under lock and key,
Yea, for a sackcloth shroud to cover me.'
But yet to me she will not do that grace,
For which full pale and withered is my face.
But, sir, in you it is no courtesy
To speak to an old man disdainfully,
Save he hath trespassed or in word or deed.
In Holy Writ ye may yourselves well read,
'In presence of an old man, hoar of head,
Ye should arise'; wherefore be counselèd,
Nor to an old man more unkindness show
Than ye would bear, when age shall shed its snow
Above your brows, if ye so long abide.
And God be with you, as ye walk or ride.
I must go thither where I have to go."

"Nay, nay, old churl. By Heaven, thou shalt not so,"
Spoke up another reveler anon.
"Thou leav'st us not so lightly, by Saint John.
Right now thou spakest of that traitor Death,
That all our friends in this land murdereth.
Then on my troth, and as thou art his spy,
Tell where he is, or dear thou shalt it buy.
I swear it by the Holy Sacrament,
For thou art of his party and art bent
On slaying us young folk, thou agèd Cain."

"Young sirs," quoth he, "if now ye are so fain
To meet with Death, turn up this crookèd way,

For in that grove I left him, sooth to say,
Under a tree and there will he abide.
Not for your boasting will he run and hide.
See ye that oak? Right there ye shall him find.
And may our Lord, that died for all mankind,
Save and amend you!" answered this old man.
And each of these three revelers then ran
Till to that tree he came, and there he found
Of florins of fine gold, coined true and round,
Wellnigh a seven bushels as they thought.
And then no longer after Death they sought,
But each of them so glad was of that sight,
Because the florins were so fine and bright,
That down they sat them by this precious hoard.
The worst of them was first to speak a word.

"Brethren," quoth he, "pay heed to what I say;
Great is my wisdom, though I jest and play.
This wealth hath Fortune given us that we
May lead our life in mirth and jollity,
And lightly as it comes so shall it go.
Eh, by the Mass! who had the wit to know
That we should have to-day so fair a grace?
But could this gold be carried from this place
Home to my house, or else to yours, or yours,—
For well ye wot that all this gold is ours, —
Then were we in supreme felicity;
But, verily, by day it may not be;
The folk would call us thieves and, for our hoard,
Would by the neck-bone hang us in a cord.
This treasure must be carried in by night
Full craftily and come to no man's sight.

So I propose that we among us all
Draw cut and see on whom the cut may fall,
And he that hath the cut shall blithely go
Away to town, nor let the grasses grow
Beneath his feet, and bring us wine and bread
Full secretly. The two of us, instead,
Shall guard the gold; and if he doth not tarry,
When it is night we will this treasure carry
Whither we all agree." Then with a twist
Of hand he caught three stems within his fist
And bade draw cut and see on whom 'twould fall.
The cut fell on the youngest of them all,
And forth unto the town he went anon,
And just as soon as he was fairly gone,
The one of them spake thus unto the other:
"Thou knowest well thou art my own sworn
brother.
Now to thy profit will I something say;
Well wottest thou our fellow is away,
And here is gold in plenty, that shall be
Divided evenly among us three.
But ne'ertheless, if I could shape it thus
That it might be divided between us,
Us two, then were it not a friendly turn?"

The other answered: "I do not discern
How this may be; he knows we have the gold.
What shall we do? what can to him be told?"

"Shall it be secret?" the first rogue replied.
"If so, the way he shall be satisfied
I'll briefly tell and bring the thing about."

"I swear," the other said, "beyond all doubt,
That on my troth I will thee not betray."

"Now," quoth the first, "thou know'st that we who
stay
Are two, and two have greater strength than one.
Look, when he is sat down, even right anon
Arise, as though in wrestling sport to strive,
And through his sides I will my dagger drive,
While thou dost struggle with him as in game,
And with thy dagger look thou do the same;
And then shall all this gold divided be,
My trusted friend, between myself and thee.
Then may we both all our desires fulfill,
And play at dice right at our own sweet will."
Thus are those graceless ones agreed to slay
The third, as ye have heard the story say.

The youngest, he who went unto the town,
Full oft in heart was rolling up and down
The beauty of these florins new and bright.

"O Lord," quoth he, "if it were so I might
Have all this treasure to myself alone,
There is no man that lives beneath the throne
Of God, should live so merry as would I."
And so at last the Fiend, our enemy,
Put in his thought that he should poison buy
Wherewith to slay his fellows. Ah, but why?
The Fiend found him in such a life of sin,
That he had leave that wandering soul to win;
For this had now become his full intent,

To slay his friends and never to repent.
And forth he goes, no longer would he tarry,
Into the town, to an apothecary,
And sought of him some poison, that he might
Destroy the rats that roamed his house by night;
And, too, there was a polecat in his yard
That slew his chickens, though he kept good
guard,
And fain he would avenge him, if he could,
Upon that sly destroyer of his brood.

The apothecary said: "And thou shalt have
A thing that — so my soul may Mary save!—
So potent is no creature, though he eat
As little of it as a grain of wheat,
Or drink of it one drop, may death escape.
Yea, die he shall, whilst thou with easy gait
Might'st walk a mile, with such a furious speed
Its work is done. This drug shall serve thy need."

This man accursed within his hand hath taken
This poison in a box and then, forsaken
Of God and all good angels, forth he ran
To the next street, and of another man,
Whom there he knew, he borrowed bottles three,
And in the two his poison pourèd he.
The third, for his own drink, full clean he kept,
For all that night, when honest people slept,
He meant to bear the gold from out that place;
And when this reveler of sorry grace
Had filled with purple wine his bottles three,
Back to his two companions wended he.

What needeth it to sermon of it more?
For just as they had planned his death before,
Right so they have him slain, and that anon;
When this was over, spake the bolder one:
"Now let us sit and drink, and make us merry,
And afterward we will his body bury";
And with that word he chose, by fatal chance,
A poisoned bottle and in ignorance
He drank of it and passed it to his friend,
For which anon their lives had sudden end.
But certes, no physician, I suppose,
Hath ever writ, in any book, of throes
More terrible, of poison-signs more true,
Than had these wretches, these assassins two,
Before their ending. So their lives were sped,
And he, their poisoner, was also dead.

O cursèd sin of utter cursedness!
O traitorous homicide! O foul excess!
O gluttony! O drink! O sin of dice!
O blasphemy, with oaths that sacrifice
The name of Christ to careless use and pride!
Alas, mankind! how may it so betide
That unto thy Creator, who thee wrought
And with His precious blood so dear thee bought,
Thou art so false and so unkind, alas!

Now may the grace of God upon you pass
And save you from the sin of avarice!
My holy pardons will ensure you bliss,
If that ye offer coins or other things,
As silver brooches, spoons, and finger-rings.

Come bow ye to the Pope, for whom I stand.
I bought my license from his holy hand.
Come, woman, give me wool, and in my roll
I'll write thy name, and heaven shall take thy soul.
Now by the mighty powers unto me lent,
All you who pay I'll wash as innocent
As ye were born.

An English Pilgrim

"Lo, pilgrims, thus I preach,
But Jesus Christ, the one true Healer, teach
You better, for the pardons that avail
Are only His, and those are not on sale.

"But, sirs, to business! One thing I forgot.
Such relics and such pardons have I, not

The Guesten Hall, Winchester, Where Pilgrims Were Lodged

A man in England with my stock may cope.
Remember that I had them of the Pope.
If any of you be in mood devout,
And would be cleansed of sin, step boldly out,
And right down here before me meekly kneel
And take my pardon, that your souls will heal
Of every ill. Or else, as on we wend,
Take pardon fresh and new at each mile's end, —
That is, provided that your pay is new
And fresh with every mile. To each of you
It is an honor in this train to have
So competent a Pardoner to save
Your souls, should any accident betide,
As ye go jaunting through the countryside;
For peradventure one or more of you
May tumble down and break his neck in two.
Look what a safety 'tis throughout the trip
That I am fallen in your fellowship,
One who can shrive you all, both high and low,

Should any soul from out the body go.
I counsel that our Host here shall begin,
For he is most envelopèd in sin.
Come forth, Sir Host, and pay thy fee anon,
And thou shalt kiss my relics every one,
Yea, for a groat. Unbuckle now thy purse."

"Nay, nay," quoth he. "Christ send on me His curse
If I do this! Thy relics grieve my nose.
Thou wouldest make me kiss thy dirty hose
And swear a saint had worn them. Get away!"

This Pardoner had not a word to say;
So angry was he that he could not speak.

"Now," quoth our Host, "no grace of thine I seek.
I'll have no dealings with an angry man."
But right anon the worthy Knight began,
Lest all the sport should end in quarrel rough.

"No more of this, for it is full enough.
Sir Pardoner, be glad and merry of cheer;
And ye, Sir Host, that are to me so dear,
Now prithee give the Pardoner a kiss.
And prithee, Pardoner, draw near for this;
And as we did before, let's laugh and play."
Anon they kissed and rode along the way.

[The Wife of Bath no longer could be hushed.
So many years it was since she had blushed,
She scrupled not to tell that cavalcade
Of all the marriages that she had made.]

The Wife of Bath

"Experience, though no authority
Were in this world, were full enough for me
In marriage sorrow to be passing sage,
For since I was, my lords, twelve year of age,—
—Thanks be to God, who saw my wishes sped!—
Five husbands at the church door have I wed,
For even so many wore the yoke for me,
And all were worthy men in their degree.
Blessèd be God, that I have wedded five!
Welcome the sixth, whenever he arrive!

"Now, sir, now will I utter forth my tale.
As ever may I drink of wine or ale,

I shall say sooth of husbands that I had,
As three of them were good and two were bad.
The three were kindly men, and rich and old,
And these in full subjection did I hold.
When they had given me their wealth and land,
I needed not, ye well may understand,
To put forth any further diligence
To win their love or do them reverence.
They doted on me so, by Heaven above,
I set no value on their easy love;
It is a woman's way to care for what
Is hard to get and what she hath not got.
But since I had them wholly in my hand,
And they to me had given their wealth and land,
Why should I be at trouble them to please
Except for mine own profit and mine ease?
I governed them so well—O Lord, the pain
I caused 'em and the woe!—that each was fain
To bring me fairings from the market-place,
And blissful was he would I smooth my face
And speak him fair, for often would I chide.
'Old barrelful of lies!' 'Old stingy-hide!'
'What ails thee, fool, to spy upon thy wife?'
'O sweet Sir Rascal, Jesu short thy life!'
'Would thunderbolt and lightningflash might break
That withered neck of thine!' 'Twas thus I spake,
For though the Pope had sat with us at board,
I would have spared them not one bitter word.
And I could feign and lie and whine and bleat,
For women's gifts are spinning, tears, deceit.
And so, by scolding or by stratagem,
At last I ever had the best of them.

"Of my fourth husband now must I aver
That this fourth husband was a reveler.
And I, still young, was wild of spirit,—yea,
Stubborn and strong and as a magpie gay.
Well could I dance until the harp would fail,
And sing, be sure, as any nightingale,
When I had drunk a draught of good sweet wine;
And so in mirth I lived that life of mine.

"Ah, my Lord Christ, when I remember me
Upon my youth and on my jollity,
It tickleth me at heart-root. Good or bad,
Still to this day my heart it maketh glad
That I have had my world, as in my time.
But poisonous Age, alas! hath stolen my prime,
Hath robbed me of my beauty and my pith.
Let go, farewell! The devil go therewith!
The flour of life is gone,—now, as I can,
I must make shift to live upon the bran,
But yet to be right merry will I seek.
And now of my fourth husband hear me speak.

"He was a reveler, but we were quits.
Against his own I set my woman's wits.
He courted other women to his loss;
I made him of that selfsame wood a cross;
For I would be so blithe in company,
In his own grease I made that gallant fry.
Saint James! on earth I was his purgatory.
For which I hope his soul is now in glory.
For God it knows, how often at my whim
He sat and sang, with his shoe pinching him.

Was none save God and he that ever knew
How sore I made the galling of his shoe.
He died when from Jerusalem I came
And lies beneath the rood-beam; but his
name
Is not writ over him with curious
Emblazonry and carving dolorous,
As royal tombs are wrought. Nay, nay, let be!
It were but waste to bury him preciously.
Farewell to him! God give his soul good rest!
He now is in his grave and coffin-chest.

"And now of my fifth husband will I tell.
God grant his soul come never into hell!
Yet he was roughest with me; many a blow
He gave; upon my ribs all in a row
I feel them yet and shall till life is gone.
Yet though the rascal beat me every bone,
Still with his beatings was my love increased.
I loved him most because he loved me least.

"Have mercy on his soul, O God above!
I took him not for riches, but for love.
An Oxford scholar once, he'd doffed his gown
And had come home to board there in our town
With Alison my gossip—God receive
Her soul!—within whose ear I used to
breathe
My husband's every secret; yea, to her,
Another, and my niece, I would transfer
All that he told me, though it were a thing
That might have cost his head in publishing.

"And so befell that once, in time of Lent,—
So often I unto my gossip went,
For ever hath it pleased me to be gay,
And walk abroad in March, April, and May,
From house to house to catch what news might fly—
This scholar, Jankin, Alison, and I
Into the fields for merry pastime went.
My husband was at London all that Lent,
And so the better chance was mine, ye ween,
To go abroad and see, and to be seen
Of lusty folk. What wist I how my lot
Might yet be cast, with whom, or in what spot?
Therefore to all church festivals I went,
Processions, preachings, and was ever bent
To go on pilgrimages, even as here.
No scripture plays I missed nor wedding cheer,
Wearing my gayest skirts of scarlet red.
These worms, these moths, these mites have never
 fed
On Sunday clothes of mine, the sooth to say.
And why? Because I wore them every day.

"Now will I tell you how it chanced with me.
I say that in the meadows sauntered we,
And passed such pleasant talk and compliment,
Jankin and I, that, always provident,
I spake to him and told him how that he,
If I were widow, then should marry me.
For certainly—in boast it is not said—
I never was without provision made
For marriage and for other matters eke.
I hold that mouse's heart not worth a leek

That only one hole hath to skurry to
And, if that fail, all hope is fallen through.

"But now, sir,—let me see—where was I then?
Aha, Saint John! I have my tale again.

"When my fourth husband was upon his bier,
I wept aloud and made me sorry cheer,
As is with widows customary case,
And with my kerchief covered o'er my face,
But since another mate I had in view,
The tears I shed, I warrant, were but few.

"Now in the morning was my husband borne
To church by neighbors that did for him mourn.
Jankin was one of them, and ye must know,
So help me God, that when I saw him go
Behind the bier, methought he had a pair
Of legs and feet so shapely and so fair
That all mine heart I gave into his hold.
He was, I trow, a twenty winter old,
And I was forty, but my heart was young,
And rich I was, and of a lively tongue,
And comely still—a lusty wife to win.
Alas, alas! that ever love was sin!

"What should I say but when the month had end,
Jankin, this scholar blithe, my gallant friend,
Had wedded me with joyous festival,
And to him gave I land and treasure all
That ever had been given me before,
But afterward repented me full sore.

He would let nothing be as I might list.
Saint James! and once he smote me with his fist,
For tearing leaf from book, so shrewd a blow
Mine ear waxed deaf, as all ye pilgrims know.
Stubborn I was as is a lioness,
A very jangler with my tongue, nor less
Than I had ever done in years before
Would I go gossiping from door to door,
However he forbade it and would prate
And musty Roman stories would relate,
As how Simplicius Gallus left his wife
And her forsook for term of all his life,
And this, upon my word, for nothing more
Than that she looked, bareheaded, out of door.

"But all for naught. I set not at a straw
Proverb or history or tale or saw,
And I would not by him corrected be.
I hate him that my vices telleth me,
And so do more of us, God wot, than I.
This made him with me wroth exceedingly;
And still I gave him better than he sent.

"Now will I tell you truly why I rent
The leaf from out his book, for which this ear
He struck so hard it never since might hear.

"He had a book that gladly day and night
He'd sit and read, still laughing for delight.
'Twas like the cardinal's book of wicked wives,
For trust me well, except it be for lives
Of saints, these scholars nothing good can say

Of women. By Saint Thomas! it is they
Who write the books and then believe them. *Who
Painted the lion?* Ha, I warrant you
Upon my troth, had women written stories,
As scholars have within their oratories,
They would have written of men more wickedness
Than all the race of Adam may redress.

"But now to tell you how it was I took
So terrible a beating for a book.
Jankin, my lord, one night sat by our fire
Reading aloud,—how Eve, for her desire
To taste an apple, brought the world to woe;
How Samson lost his hair; and ever so
He read of mischief wrought by womankind,
Xantippe, Clytemnestra, till my mind
Was all a-chafe—right as the rogue designed—
But this of all most grievous did I find,—
How once a Roman, one Latumyus,
Complained unto his fellow Arrius,
That in his garden grew a certain tree,
On which, he said, his wives, one, two, and three,
Had for vexation hanged themselves and died.
'O dear my brother,' Arrius replied,
'Give me a graft of that same blessèd tree
And in my garden planted it shall be.'

"And then of wives of later date he read,—
How some have slain their husbands in their bed;
And some have driven nails into the brain
Of sleeping husbands who have thus been slain;
And some have poisoned husbands in their drink.

He spake more harm than any heart may think.
Therewith he knew more proverbs, to my wrath,
Than this green planet herbs and grasses hath.
'Better it is,' this Jankin quoth, 'for men
To dwell in lion's lair or dragon's den
Than with a scolding woman to abide.'
And while I heard us women so belied,
Who could conceive what pain I had and woe!

"And when I saw he would sit reading so
Within this cursèd book the livelong night,
All suddenly, as there he read, for spite
Three leaves from out of it away I tore
And with my fist I struck him, furthermore,
So lustily that down into the fire
Backward he fell; then up he sprang, with ire
As fierce as any lion, and my head
He smote so mightily I lay as dead.
And when this scholar saw how still I lay,
He was aghast and would have fled his way,
But finally out of my swoon I woke:
'O hast thou slain me, robber?' so I spoke.
'Even for my land thus hast thou murdered me?
Yet, ere I die, I'd give a kiss to thee.'

"And near he came and gently kneeled upon
The floor and said: 'Dear sister Alison,
So help me God, I'll never smite thee more;
Thy fault it is I did so heretofore.
Forgive it me, I pray thee.' Soft and meek
He spake, and yet I hit him on the cheek
And said: 'Aha! so far avenged am I.

Now can I speak no more, now will I die.'
And so at last, and after much ado,
A settlement was reached between us two.
He gave the bridle wholly to my hand
To have the government of house and land,
And of his tongue and fist. The rule I took,
And first of all I made him burn his book.
And after I had thus secured to me
The lordship of our realm by victory,
And he had said: 'My own true, loyal wife,
Do as thou likest, even all thy life,
Be guardian of thyself and of my store,'—
After that day we never quarreled more.
I was as kind to him, once disciplined,
As any wife from Denmark unto Inde,
And also true, and so was he to me.
I pray to God, that sits in majesty,
To bless his soul, out of His mercy dear.
Now will I tell my tale, if ye will hear."

The Friar laughed out when he had heard all this.
"Now, dame," quoth he, "now as I hope for bliss,
This is a long preamble of a tale."

Then must the Summoner begin to rail
Upon the Friar. "Zounds!" quoth he. "Give o'er!
A friar must be meddling evermore.
Friar and fly will fall in every dish.
Preambulacion! now what might he wish
To say by that long word? Amble or trot,
Stand still or sit thee down, it matters not.
Thou hinderest our pastime as we ride."

"Yea, wilt thou so, Sir Summoner?" replied
The Friar. "By my faith, before I go
I'll tell a tale of Summoners, and so
That all this folk shall laugh, to thy disgrace."

The Friar

The Summoner returned: "Beshrew thy face!
Yea, and beshrew myself, but if I tell
Such tales of friars ere our thirst we quell
At Sittingbourne, where pilgrims halt to dine,
That I shall make to grieve that heart of thine,
For well I wot thy patience soon is gone."

Our Host then shouted: "Peace! and that anon!"
He added: "Let the woman tell her tale.
Ye fare as folk that drunken are of ale.
Do, dame, speak out your story; that is best."

"All ready, sir," quoth she, "were I but blest
With favor of this worthy Friar here."

"Yes, dame," quoth he. "Tell on, and I will hear."

[And so, with sundry hits at friars, who
Now walk the world as fairies used to do,—
And hardly is the green earth better for
The change,—she told about a bachelor

A Pilgrim Rest House

Of Arthur's court, who wed a beggar-wife,
An ugly crone, in ransom of his life;
For he, on peril of his head, must say
What women love the best, and when the day

Of doom had come, and he was seeking still,
She told him that they love to have their will;
And for that word he plighted her his troth
And wedded her, albeit he was full loth
To take that low-born beldam by the hand;
But sagely gave she him to understand
That gentlehood comes not of long descent
Nor riches, but of virtuous intent:
"Who seeks to do all gentle deeds he can,
Take him to be the greatest gentleman.
Christ would, we claim of Him our gentleness."
In poverty no shame would she confess:
"Glad poverty is honorable; he
Who lightly bears the load of poverty,
I hold him rich, though not a shirt he hath,
For poverty goes singing on its path."
As for old age and ugliness, behold,
Enchanted had she been on fairy wold,
And at his kiss she was as lovely seen
As any lady, yea, as any queen
'Twixt east and west; and when the knight saw this,
His heart was bathèd in a bath of bliss.]

"And thus they lived together till life's end
In perfect joy; and Jesu Christ us send
Husbands both young and meek, and grace to tarry
A longer time in life than those we marry.
Especially I pray Christ short their lives
That will not be submissive to their wives;
And cross old niggards, clutching at their pence,
God send them soon the very pestilence."

Now while the Wife was telling of her tale,
This noble Frair, though manners did not fail
So far that he by speech broke in on her,
Was glowering always on the Summoner;
But when she ceased he said unto the Wife:
"Dame," quoth he, "may God give you right good life!
Your tale, methinks, is better than your views.
Now if it may this company amuse,
I of a Summoner will make my game.

The Summoner

Forsooth, ye well may gather from the name
That of a Summoner no pleasant thing
May one relate; so be not murmuring.
A Summoner's a runner up and down
On errands vile, beaten in every town.
No story of a Summoner is sweet."

Our Host said: "Ah, sir, ye should be discreet
And courteous, as beseemeth the estate

Of clergy; we will have no sharp debate.
Tell us your tale and let the Summoner be."

"Nay," quoth the Summoner, "let him say to me
Whatso he list, and when it comes my turn,
By all the saints, I'll make his ears to burn.
Oh, I shall tell him what an honor 'tis
To beg from door to door with pious phiz
And wheedling purr, like to a hungry cat."

Our Host replied: "Peace, peace! no more of that!"
And to the Friar said with friendly cheer:
"Tell us your tale, my gracious master dear."

[Forthwith the Friar told how it befell
A Summoner to swear, as fitted well,
Leal brotherhood unto the Fiend, and dwell
Forever in his cursèd house of hell.]

This Summoner high in his stirrups stood.
As when a wind goes through an aspen-wood,
So trembled he for very rage and ire.

"My lords," quoth he, "but one thing I desire.
I do beseech you of your courtesy,
As ye have sat and heard this Friar lie,
There be to me the like attention shown.
And may God bless you all, save him alone!"

[Then pictured he a friar, with staff and scrip
And gown tucked high, false smiles upon his lip,
Prying about from village door to door,
Begging for meal, for cheese, for corn, and more.

"Give us a bushel of your wheat or rye,
An Easter cake, a cheese, a pigeon-pie;
Or give us what ye list, a silver penny,
A slice of ham, so be that ye have any,
A strip of this warm blanket, gentle dame,

The Grey Friars, Canterbury

Our sister dear, and your belovèd name
In ivory tablets shall my pencil grave,—
Bacon or beef or whatsoe'er ye have."
The story told how where this friar thought
To practice knavery, himself was caught

By such a trick as covered him with scorn.
And with that tale they came to Sittingbourne.

By dinner was this quarrel somewhat eased,
But since the gentlefolk seemed little pleased
With these last tales, our Host, when once again
We took the road, looked sharply down the train
To find a speaker of more holy bent,
Who yet should not forswear all merriment.]
"Sir Clerk of Oxford," Harry Bailly said,
"Ye ride as coy and still as is a maid,
At her first bridal, sitting at the board.
This day I've heard not of your tongue a word.
Some problem deep I trow you ponder on,
But 'time for everything,' saith Solomon.
Prithee, look up and be of better cheer.
It is no time to muse and study here.
Tell us some merry tale to short the way,
For when a man is entered in a play,
He needs must bear his part with blithe assent.
But preach ye not, as friars do in Lent,
To make us for our old transgressions weep;
And see your story put us not to sleep.
Tell us some merry thing adventurous.
Your scholar rhetoric is not for us.
Keep that in store until ye would endite
High style, as when men unto monarchs write;
But speak so plain at this time, we you pray,
That we may understand the words you say."

This worthy Clerk benignantly replied:
"I am beneath your rod the while we ride.

Ye have the government upon the way,
And therefore, Host, your hest will I obey,
As far, forsooth, as reason may comply.
I will a story tell to you that I
At Padua learned from Francis Petrarch, he

The Clerk of Oxenford

Whose poetry illumed all Italy.
He is now dead and nailèd in his chest.
I pray to God to give his soul good rest."

TALE OF THE CLERK OF OXFORD

PART I

On the west side of Italy there lies,
Down at the foot of Vesulus the cold,
A lusty plain and fruitful, where thine eyes
Full many a town and castle may behold,
Founded in time of our forefathers old,
And many another sight of joy and fame;
Salùces this fair country is by name.

A marquis once held lordship of that land,
As had his ancestors in years gone by.
Obedient and ready to his hand
Were all his leal retainers, low and high.
Thus in delight he lived beneath the sky,
Beloved and feared, through Fortune's steadfast grace,
By lesser lords and common populace.

Therewith he was, to speak of his descent,
The gentlest born throughout all Lombardy;
Fair, strong, and young, of sober government,
And full of honor and of courtesy;
So wise his country on him might rely,—
Save in some matters where he was to blame—
And Walter was this youthful noble's name.

For this I blame him — he considered naught
What might in coming time to him betide,
But on his present sport was all his thought,
To hunt and hawk throughout the countryside.
Well-nigh all other business he let slide;
And eke he would not — which was worst of all —
Wed him a wife, for aught that might befall.

This point so grievously his people bore
That in a flock one day they to him went,
And one of them that wisest was of lore —
Or else because the lord best gave consent
That he should tell him what his people meant,
Or that he could such matters make most clear, —
Unto the marquis said as ye shall hear:

"O noble marquis, your humanity
Gives us this faith and courage we possess,
As often as there is necessity
To tell to you our grief and our distress.
And now, lord, suffer of your gentleness
That we with piteous heart to you complain,
Nor let your ears my humble voice disdain.

"Although the matter toucheth me no more
Than any other man here in this place,
Yet insomuch as ye, dear lord, before
Have shown me favor and continual grace,
I dare the better ask of you a space
Of audience, to set forth our request,
And ye, my lord, do what to you seems best.

"For certès, lord, so pleasing unto us
Are you and all your deeds, and ever were,
Thought might not frame a lot more prosperous,
For all things in our happiness concur
Save only one; if but, most gracious sir,
Ye would be wed, then were our wishes blest,
Then were your people's hearts in sovereign rest.

"Oh, bow your neck beneath that blissful yoke
Of sovereignty, nowise of servitude,
Which is called marriage among Christian folk;
And in your wisdom be it understood
Our days pass by, in fashion ill or good,
For though we sleep or wake, or roam or ride,
Still fleets the time; for none will it abide.

"And though with you green youth is yet in flower,
Age creepeth on it ever, still as stone;
Death menaceth all life and, at his hour,
Smites each estate, for there escapeth none;
And all as certain as we know each one
That we shall die, uncertain are we all
What day and how shall death upon us fall.

"Therefore accept of us the true intent,
That never yet refused your high behest,
And we will, lord, so be that ye consent,
Choose you a wife with swift and happy quest,
Born of the gentlest blood and of the best
In all this land, so that the bond should seem
Honor to God and you, as plain folk deem.

"From out this busy fear our hearts have hid
Deliver us and wed, for God's dear sake;
For should it so befall, as God forbid,
That through your death your noble line should break,
And this your heritage a stranger take,
O woe to us for all the rest of life!
Wherefore we pray you, quickly wed a wife."

Their meek entreaty and their anxious mien
Moved pity in the marquis' heart. Said he:
"Mine own dear people, to an unforeseen,
Unwished-for course ye are constraining me.
I have delighted in my liberty,
But seldom found in marriage; and ye would
This freedom I exchange for servitude.

"But ne'ertheless, I see your true intent,
And trust your wisdom in my wonted way;
And so of my free will do I consent
To marry and as soon as ever I may;
But in that ye have offered me this day
To choose a wife for me, I do release
You from that choice, and beg that offer cease.

"For, God knows, children, to their parents' pain,
Are oft unlike their worthy ancestors.
Goodness comes all of God, not of the strain
From which they spring. So, kindly counselors,
I put my trust in Him, Who goodness pours
On whom He will. My marriage, state, and rest
I leave to Him to do as seems Him best.

"Let me alone in choosing me a wife;
That load on mine own back I will endure;
But I you pray and charge upon your life
That, whatso wife I take, ye promise sure
To worship her, while life may last, with your
Best service, word and deed and heart's desire,
As if she had an emperor for sire.

"And, furthermore, this shall ye swear, that ye
Against my choice shall grumble not nor strive;
For since I shall forego my liberty
At your request, then, as I hope to thrive,
There where my heart is set, there will I wive;
And if to this ye will not give consent,
Press me no more with marriage argument."

Right heartily they swore and well agreed
To all this thing; no mortal said him nay;
Yet ere they went for one more grace must plead,—
That he will name to them the certain day
Of bridal and the earliest he may;
For yet the people had a secret dread
That after all this marquis would not wed.

He named the day which suited him the best,
On which he would be wed, if God should please,
And said he did all this at their request,
And they, with grateful mind and heart at ease,
Full reverently kneeling on their knees,
Gave thanks to him, and thus this folk had won
The end they sought and wended home anon.

And hereupon he bade his officers
To make provision for the wedding feast,
And to his household knights, and squires whose spurs
Were yet to earn, to greatest and to least
Gave divers charges, so that never ceased
The running to and fro, for all would pay
Full honor to their master's marriage-day.

PART II

Not far from that majestic palace which
This marquis planned with wedding mirth to grace,
There stood a hamlet, in all beauty rich
That vale and river yield, but hard the case
Of those poor folk that there had dwelling place,
Keeping their beasts and, when their labors sped,
Bringing from out the earth their daily bread.

Among these poor folk lived a certain man
Who was accounted poorest of them all,
But high God, when He will, His blessing can
Send down into a little oxen.stall,
Janicula, the hamlet did him call.
One child he had abiding with him there,
A maid, Griselda, young and passing fair.

But as for beauty that in virtue lies,
One of the fairest was she under sun,
For poverty had made her early wise,
And through her heart no vain desires had run.
Full oftener her drinking had been done
From well than wineglass; to her duty true,
Labor, not idle ease, her girlhood knew.

But though of tender age was this fair maid,
Yet in the breast of her virginity
Enclosèd was a spirit ripe and staid,
And in great reverence and charity
Her poor old feeble father fostered she;
A few sheep, spinning as she watched, she kept
Out in the fields, nor rested till she slept.

When she came home at dusk, she oft would bring
Such roots and herbs as on the way she found,
And these would shred and seethe for nourishing
Her father and herself; hard as the ground
She made her bed, but, as in duty bound,
Sustained her father's life from day to day
With every service that a child may pay.

Part of the Tithe Barn, Maidstone

Upon Griselda, on this simple lass,
Full often had this marquis cast his eye,
As he, in hunting, field or cot might pass,
And when it chanced he did the maid espy,
He looked upon her, as he galloped by,
Not with the idle gallantry of youth,
But honoring her in soberness and truth,

Commending in his heart her womanhood,
And virtue such as never was before
In one so young; all people called her good,
And though the peasantry have little lore
And insight as to virtue, still he bore
Their words in mind and so determinèd
To wed but her, if ever he should wed.

The day of wedding came, but not a soul
Could tell what woman was to be the bride;
So strange it was men hardly could control
Their wonder and alarm, but said aside:
"Will not the marquis by his word abide?
Will he not wed? alas! alas the while!
Why will he thus himself and us beguile?"

But yet the marquis hath had craftsmen make
Of jewels set in azure and in gold,
Brooches and rings, for this Griselda's sake,
And measure took for garments manifold
By means of maiden like to her in mould;
And hath provided those adornments all
That appertain to wedding festival.

And now the mid-forenoon of this same day
Approacheth, when the wedding is to be;
The palace all was put in fair array,
Hall, chambers, every room in its degree;
In pantries and in butteries one might see
Great store of dainty victual, fetched from far
Where Italy's remotest reaches are.

This royal marquis, splendidly arrayed,
With lords and ladies in his company
Whom to attend the bridal he had prayed,
Followed by knights who yet went marriage-free,
With many a sound of sundry melody,
In festal wise hath ta'en the shortest road
To that poor hamlet which I lately showed.

Griselda, innocent, God wot, that on
Her own behalf is made this grand array,
To bring in water from the well is gone,
And cometh home as soon as ever she may,
For she had heard it said that on this day
The marquis should be wed, and if she might,
She fain would see a little of that sight.

She thought: "With other maids who dwell hard by,
My fellows, in our door I'll stand and see
The marchioness, and therefore will I try
To do at home as quickly as may be
The labor which belongeth unto me;
And then I may at leisure view the bride,
If she this way unto the castle ride."

And as she would within her door be gone,
The marquis came and after her did call,
And she set down her waterpot anon
Beside the threshold in an ox's stall,
And down upon her knees made speed to fall,
And with grave countenance she kneeleth still,
Till she hath heard this lord declare his will.

The thoughtful marquis spake unto this maid
Full soberly and courteously: "Where,
Griselda, is your father?" So he said,
And she, with reverent and humble air,
Replied: "My lord, within our cottage there";
And in she goeth without hindrance more
And led her father forth from out the door.

The marquis by the hand took this old man
And said, when he had drawn him well aside,
"Janicula, I neither would nor can
A longer time my heart's glad purpose hide.
If thou vouchsafe, then, whatsoe'er betide,
Thy daughter will I take, before I wend,
To be my wife until her life shall end.

"Thou lovest me, as well believe I may,
For thou my faithful liege art born and bred,
And all that pleaseth me, I well dare say,
To thee is pleasing; tell me without dread
Thy mind on this which I to thee have said,—
If my desire consent from thee doth draw
To take a marquis for thy son-in-law."

This sudden hap this man astonished so
That red he waxed and all abashed he stood,
And from his quaking lips could hardly flow
These words, no more: "My lord, that which I would
Is what ye will; what seemeth to you good
I question not, ye be my lord so dear;
Right as ye list dispose this matter here."

Then quoth this marquis softly: "Yet would I
That in thy chamber I and thou and she
Hold conference; and dost thou gather why?
Her I would ask if her own will it be
To pass beneath my rule and marry me.
And all this in thy presence shall be done.
Apart from thee disclosure shall be none."

While in the chamber these three were about
Their covenant, as ye shall shortly hear,
The people pressed into the yard without
And wondered at the comfort and the cheer
In which Griselda kept her father dear;
But wonder most of all Griselda might,
For never yet had she beheld such sight.

No wonder is it though amazed she were
To see so great a guest come in that place.
Such guests had ne'er been entertained of her,
And hence she looked on him with paling face.
But that the tale may move at swifter pace,
These are the words that there the marquis said
Unto this gentle, true, devoted maid:

"Griselda," said he, "ye must understand
It pleaseth both your father here and me
That you in marriage yield to me your hand;
And I suppose ye will it so to be;
But first 'tis fitting I demand," quoth he,
"Since all so hastily this knot is knit,
Will ye assent or would ye think on it?

"And further, are ye ready with good heart
To do my will, so that I freely may
At mine own pleasure make you laugh or smart,
And never you my mood or whim gainsay?
And still when I say 'yea,' ye say not 'nay,'
Neither by spoken word nor frowning brow?
Swear this, and then I swear our marriage-vow."

Wondering upon this word, quaking for dread,
She answered: "Lord, unworthy and unfit
Am I for this great honor you to wed;
But what ye wish yourself, so wish I it,
And here I swear I will to you submit,
Nor ever disobey you. Rather I
Would lose my life, though I were loth to die."

"This is enough, Griselda mine." quoth he,
And forth he goeth with full sober cheer
Out at the door, and after him came she,
And to the people spake he firm and clear.
"This is my wife," quoth he, "that standeth here.
Let whoso loveth me, love her, I pray,
And honor her; there is no more to say."

And that no remnant of her life of care
She should into his palace bring, he bade
That women should unclothe her then and there,
Whereat these ladies were not over-glad
To touch those poor coarse garments that she had;
But yet this maid, of beauty passing bright,
From foot to head they clad in bridal white.

They've combed her shining hair, that lay untressed
In peasant wise, and with their fingers frail
A coronet upon her head have pressed
And showered her with jewels thick as hail.
Of her array why should I make a tale?
Scarcely the neighbors knew her, scarce her sire,
Transfigured by such splendid rich attire.

This marquis hath espoused her with a ring
Brought for the purpose, and his bride hath set
On snow-white, easy-ambling horse to bring
Her to the palace, without further let
Or hindrance. And his joyous people met
And led her in, and thus the day went by
In revelry till sunset flushed the sky.

And that this story move at swifter pace,
I say that to this new-made marchioness
God hath such favor given of His grace,
That none who looked on her would ever guess
She had been born and bred a shepherdess,
And dwelt in cottage or in oxen-stall;
She seemed one nurtured in a royal hall.

To every wight she waxed so passing dear
And worshipful, that folk where she was born,
Who from her birth had known her year by year,
Would scarce believe 'twas she, but durst have sworn
That this no daughter was of that forlorn
Old man Janicula; she seemed to them
Another creature with her diadem.

For although ever virtuous was she,
She had increased in such high excellence
Of goodness, set in gracious dignity,
And so discreet had grown, with eloquence
So sweet and worthy of all reverence,
And could so win all hearts by gentle grace,
That each one loved her who beheld her face.

Not only in Salùces did men quote
The wisdom of her words and praise her name,
But eke in many a region far remote.
If one spake well of her, there said the same
Another and another, till her fame
Was spread so wide that folk both young and old
Flock to Saluce Griselda to behold.

And thus this Walter, who had wed so low,—
Nay, with good fortune, well and royally—
In God's peace liveth, while the seasons go,
And outward happiness enough had he.
And since he saw that under low degree
Was often virtue hid, folk held him wise,
The most sagacious lord beneath the skies.

Not only had this sweet Griselda wit
To know all ways of wifely homeliness,
But also, when the case required it,
The public good she could subserve no less;
There was no rancor, strife nor any stress
In all the country she could not appease
And bring all to contentment and to ease.

Although her husband absent were, the while
High folk and others of the land fell out,
Her words would those opponents reconcile,
So sage her speech, so earnest and devout;
Her judgments put all questions out of doubt.
Men deemed her sent from heaven to be their friend
And all their wrongs and troubles to amend.

It was not long ere this Griselda bore
A child,—a daughter, as the chance befell,
And though a little son had pleased her more,
Glad was the marquis and the folk, for well
They knew another tale might be to tell
Some other day; although the maid came first,
A boy might follow; best comes after worst.

PART III

There came unto this lord, as oft hath come
To other husbands, were the fact confessed,
A restless longing, strange and burdensome,
The true devotion of his wife to test.
Though yet the child had lain upon her breast
But little time, this marquis craved to try
(All needlessly, God wot) her constancy.

He'd put her to the proof enough before
And found her ever good,— what needed it
To tempt her so, and always more and more?
Though some men praise it for a subtle wit,
For me, I say it doth but ill befit
A husband to torment a faithful wife
Till dread and anguish darken all her life.

Now to his end this path the marquis took.
He came to her one night, there where she lay;
Alone he came, with stern and troubled look,
And spake: "Griselda," thus quoth he, "that day
When I from poverty took you away
And raised you to estate of nobleness,
That day ye've not forgotten, as I guess.

"I say, Griselda, that this dignity
To which I have exalted you, I trow
Maketh you not forgetful how to me
Ye came from an estate full poor and low,
Whatever happiness ye now may know.
Give heed to every word I say to you;
There is no wight that heareth save us two.

"Ye wot yourself full well how ye came here
Into this house; it is not long ago;
And though to me ye precious are and dear,
Unto my gentles ye be nothing so;
They say to them it is great shame and woe
To render homage to a peasant born,
Sprung from that hamlet wretched and forlorn.

"And most since this thy daughter's birth have they
Spoken these words, as I must needs confess.
Now would I, as before our marriage-day,
Live with my folk in peace and quietness.
I may not to their plaint be pitiless.
With this thy daughter I am forced to deal,
Not as I would, but for my people's weal.

"And yet, God wot, full grievous 'tis to me,
And not without your knowledge will I stir
To do this thing; but this I ask," quoth he,
"Ye give me your consent to deal with her
As I deem best, nor at my doom demur.
Show now that patience which ye promisèd
And swore to me the day when we were wed."

When she had heard all this, she changed no whit
In countenance nor manner nor in tone.
One would have thought she was not grieved by it.
She said: "My child and I, lord, are your own.
All lies in your good pleasure. Ye alone
Have right and power your blood to save or spill;
All ours is yours; do with us as ye will.

"There can be nothing — so may God me save! —
Which gives you pleasure that mine heart would rue,
For there is nothing I desire to have,
Nothing I fear to lose save only you.
This is my will, to your will leal and true.
No length of time, nor death, may this remove,
Nor change the temper of my steadfast love."

Glad was this marquis of her answering,
But yet, forsooth, he feigned to be not so.
With gloomy look, as musing on a thing
Of horror, did he from her chamber go;
And shortly after, though the time was slow
To her, he secretly told his intent
Unto a man whom to his wife he sent.

A sort of sergeant was this secret man
Whom many a time before the marquis had
Found faithful in great things. To such folk can
Safely be trusted missions good or bad.
The lord knew well that whatsoe'er he said
This man would do. The case made clear to him,
He stalked into the chamber, still and grim.

"Madame," he said, "ye now must pardon me
Although I do the deed upon me laid.
Ye are so wise that very well know ye
Great lords' commandments have to be obeyed.
Well may lamenting and complaint be made,
But men must do the bidding of their lords,
And so will I; no need of further words.

"This child my orders are to bear away,"—
And spake no more, but angry brows he bent,
And roughly seized the child, as if to slay
It then, before he from the chamber went.
To all Griselda must perforce consent,
And as a lamb she sitteth meek and still,
And lets this cruel sergeant do his will.

Ill-boding was the sergeant's evil fame,
Ill-boding was his face, his speech, his air.
Ill-boding was the time in which he came.
Alas, her child, her darling, her despair!
She weened he would have slain it even there.
But ne'ertheless no tear nor moan escaped;
Unto the marquis' will, her will she shaped.

But at the last to speak this wife began
And meekly she unto the sergeant prayed
That as he was a worthy, gentle man,
She yet once more might kiss her little maid
Before it died. Then on her breast she laid
The child and, as in gladder hours than this,
Hushed it with lullaby and many a kiss.

And thus with gentle voice she spoke her loss:
"Farewell, my child, whom I no more shall see.
But since I now have signed thee with the cross
Of Christ thy Father, blesséd may He be,
The Crucified, who died for thee and me.
Thy soul, my little one, may Jesu take,
For thou to-night shalt perish for my sake."

I trow that to a nurse at such a pass
It had been hard this piteous sight to see.
Well might a mother then have cried "Alas!"
But all so true and strong of soul was she
That she endured the pang and quietly
Gave back the child and to the sergeant said:
"Have here again your little helpless maid.

"Go now," quoth she, "and do my lord's behest;
But one thing will I pray you of your grace,—
Unless my lord forbade you, lay at rest
This little body in some burial place
Where beasts nor birds may tear it nor deface."
Yet he no word to that effect would say,
But took the child and went upon his way.

This sergeant came unto his lord again
And of Griselda's words and steadfast cheer
He told him point for point, concise and plain,
And him presented with his daughter dear.
A little ruthful was this lord to hear,
But ne'ertheless his purpose held he still,
As these lords do when set upon their will;

And bade his sergeant that he secretly
This child in folds of cloth should softly wrap,
With needments all, and bear it tenderly
Within a coffer, safe as in a lap;
But, would he keep his own head from mishap,
Take full good heed he let no mortal know
From whence he came nor whither he would go;

But to Bologna, to his sister dear,
The Countess of Panago, he should take
The child, and tell her all, and pray her rear
The maiden in all gentleness, for sake
Of their own childhood hand in hand, yet make
Disclosure of the parentage to none,
Whate'er might happen as the years went on.

The sergeant goes and hath fulfilled this thing,
But to the marquis now return must we,
For busy is he with imagining
What in his wife's demeanor he may see,
Or in her words perceive of change, but he
Could never, not for all his searching, find
Her aught but gentle, dutiful, and kind.

As glad, as humble, and as busy in
All winsome ways of service and of love
As this Griselda had beforetime been
So was she still; no sudden chance might move
Her lips to name her daughter, or reprove
His deed; in earnest talk or tender game,
She never named to him her daughter's name.

PART IV

So passed four years ere had she, by God's grace,
Once more a child upon her breast to fold,—
A man-child with his father in his face,
Well-formed and fair and gracious to behold.
And when these tidings were to Walter told,
Not only he, but all his country, raised
Rejoicing for an heir and God they praised.

The child was weaned, a toddling two-year-old,
When to this marquis came, one idle day,
A fresh desire to test that wife of gold,
To see if he could tempt her to dismay
Or wrath or grief. Oh, needless to assay
Such love as hers, but husbands know no bound
When such a patient creature they have found.

"Wife," quoth the marquis, "ye have heard ere this
How that my people bear our marriage ill,
And since my son is born, more bitter is
Their murmur, that my very heart doth kill;
The voice of their complaining louder still
Comes to mine ears, till the incessant smart
Hath well-nigh slain my courage and my heart.

"Now say they thus: 'When Walter shall be gone,
Blood of Janicula must then succeed
And be our lord, for other have we none.'
Such is my people's grievance and, indeed,
Well ought I to such murmuring give heed;
Such discontent no ruler may disdain,
Although it be not spoken full and plain.

"I fain would live in peace, if but I might,
Wherefore my thought to this decision grows,—
As with his sister erst I dealt by night,
Right so of him to secretly dispose.
I give you warning, lest such sudden blows
Should startle you from out your self-control.
Be patient, I entreat, and firm of soul."

"I have," quoth she, "said thus and ever shall,—
I have no will but yours nor count as pain
What gives you joy. It grieves me not at all
Although my daughter and my son be slain
At your command, albeit of children twain
My only part was sickness and the throe
At first, and afterward a keener woe.

"Ye are our lord; then do ye with your own
Right as ye list; no counsel ask of me;
For as I left my peasant raiment thrown
Upon our cottage floor, right so," quoth she,
"Left I my will and all my liberty
And took your clothing, on our marriage-day.
Perform your own good pleasure; I obey.

"And certes, could I know your will before
'Twas spoken, I would do it every whit,
But now I wot what fate ye have in store
For this my man-child, I will further it
As if ye did to us a benefit;
For wist I that my death would do you ease,
Right gladly would I die my lord to please;

"For there is no comparison between
Death and your love,'' and when this nobleman
Beheld Griselda's constancy serene,
He drops his eyes and wonders that she can
Suffer in patience all his bitter plan;
And forth he goes with dreary countenance,
Yet doth his heart for very pleasure dance.

This ugly sergeant, in the selfsame wise
That he her daughter seized, right so hath he,
Or in worse fashion, could he worse devise,
Snatched up her son at play beside her knee.
And still so patient and so meek was she,
No sign of sorrow to her pang confessed
As soft she kissed her son and softly blessed,

Save this: she prayed the sergeant, if he might,
To lay her little son in earthy grave,
His tender limbs, so delicate to sight,
From rending fowls and snarling beasts to save,
But not a word of answer might she have.
He went his way, as heedless of her prayer,
But to Bologna brought the boy with care.

This marquis wondered ever more and more
At her unshaken patience, and if he
Had not in sooth perceived and known before
That perfectly her children lovèd she,
He would have weened that out of cruelty
Or malice or some subtle sly disguise,
She had endured all this with tranquil eyes.

But well he knew that, though she loved him best,
She loved her children next in every wise.
And now of women would I ask what test
Was needed further: might not these suffice?
What more could stubborn husband yet devise
To prove her wifehood or her steadfastness,
And he remaining still so merciless?

But there are folk of such a temper that,
When they a fixed determination take,
They cannot leave it, but keep tugging at
Their purpose as if bound unto a stake,
And nothing can their resolution break.
Right so this marquis was completely bent
On carrying out his cruel first intent.

He waited long to see if word or glance
Would show her heart had changed at all toward him,
But never found he sign of variance,
The same in face and bearing. Every whim
Of his she made her duty, nor grew dim
The love within her look. As time went by,
Still did the years her wifehood beautify.

It seemed as if there was between those two
Only one will, for still she acquiesced
In everything that Walter wished to do
And, God be thanked, it all was for the best.
Well proved she for no worldly vain unrest
Should any wife in earthly joys or ills
Will aught herself but what her husband wills.

The slander about Walter wide was spread
That of a cruel heart he wickedly,
Because a peasant woman he had wed,
Had murdered both his children privily.
Such murmur was abroad now commonly.
It was not strange, for to the people's ear
There came no word but that they murdered were.

For which, whereas his people hitherto
Had loved him well, this slanderous ill-fame
Brought him the hate to such offenses due.
To be a murderer is a hateful name.
But not for frank reproach nor muttered blame
Would he give up the purpose of his life,
For all his mind was set to prove his wife.

When now his daughter's years to twelve had grown,
Unto the court of Rome — in secret wise
Informed of his intention — he made known
His will that they should certain bulls devise,
Such as to his stern purpose may suffice,
Bidding this marquis, for his land's repose,
Take him another wife, if so he chose.

I say, he ordered made a counterfeit
Of the Pope's bulls, to this effect and scope,—
That his first marriage was annulled by it,
Even by the dispensation of the Pope,—
And this was done in the most holy hope
To heal the breach which did from him divide
His people. This was published far and wide.

The simple folk believed — and little blame
To them — that all the bull declared was so,
But when these tidings to Griselda came,
I warrant that her heart was full of woe,
But steadfast still it was to undergo
All shifts of fortune, humble now as ever,
With love that from her lord no pain could sever.

Waiting as always on the sovereign pleasure
Of him to whom her faithful heart she gave,
Of him who was her only worldly treasure,
Her very all in all. But time to save,
I tell you briefly that he so did crave
To probe her to the deepest, sorest spot,
He to Bologna wrote his subtle plot.

He prayed the earl who had his sister wed
That he bring home in all becoming state
Those children whom the people deemed were dead;
But his entreaty most of all laid weight
On secrecy,— that he communicate
To none, though many lips be question-laden,
Who was the father of this lad and maiden,

But say, the maiden came to be the bride
Of the Marquis of Salùces. And upon
This letter, was the earl so prompt to ride
That at the set of day the troop is gone
Forth toward Salùces, nobles many a one
In rich array, this maiden to escort,
Her little brother by her, proud of port.

Robed for her bridal was this fresh young maid,
Adorned with gems of colors pure and clear.
Her brother, too, was daintily arrayed,
As suited with a child of seven year;
And thus in splendor, making merry cheer,
Through Italy they ride upon their way,
Advancing toward Salùces day by day.

PART V

Meanwhile, after his wonted wicked way,
This marquis, yet his wife to tempt the more,
Even to her spirit's uttermost assay,
To learn if love were sound unto the core,
And patience still as steadfast as before,
One day, the presence-chamber thronged with folk,
To her full loudly and full rudely spoke.

"Certes, Griselda, I was well content
To marry you because I knew you good
And true and faithful and obedient,
Although no wealth ye had nor noble blood;
But in great lordship, rightly understood,
Great servitude there is of sundry kind,
As now in very soothfastness I find.

"I may not do as every ploughman may, —
My people are constraining me to take
Another wife; they clamor day by day;
And eke the Pope, their rancorous wrath to slake,
Consenteth to it for the country's sake;
And verily this much to you I'll say,
My new wife is already on her way.

"Be strong of heart and step down from her place,
And as for all that dower ye brought to me,
Take it again; I grant it of my grace.
Return unto your father's house," quoth he.
"No one may always have prosperity.
With even heart I counsel you to bear
This stroke of Fortune, nor embrace despair."

And she with patience and all reverence
Replied: "My lord, I know and I have known
Even from the first, that your magnificence
From this my poverty a spacious zone
Sunders in sooth beyond comparison;
I never held me fit, so God me aid,
To be your wife, no, nor your chambermaid.

"And in this splendid palace where ye bade
That I be mistress, may the high God bless
My soul and with His favor make me glad,
As ne'er I deemed me lady, though my dress
Were silk, but servant to your worthiness;
And more than any earthly creature, I
Will serve and love you till the day I die.

"That ye so long, of your benignity,
Have kept me thus in honor and estate
Too high for my deserts, upon my knee
I thank my God and you, and soon or late
May He reward you; now I leave your gate
And to my father's cottage gladly wend
To dwell with him until my life hath end.

"Where I was fostered as a little child,
There until death my quiet life I'll lead,
A faithful widow, ever undefiled
By other love, for since to you indeed
I gave my youth, may God forbid I heed,
I who have been the wife of such a lord,
From any other man beseeching word.

"And as for your new wife, God of His grace
Shed on you joy and all prosperity,
For I will gladly yield to her my place,
In which full blissful I was wont to be;
For since it pleaseth you, my lord," quoth she,
"You, who were all the comfort of my heart,
That I shall go, I willingly depart.

"But for your offer to restore such dower
As first I brought, it well is in my mind
I had no more than wretched clothes that hour
Ye chose me, — clothes it now were hard to find.
O God, good God, how gentle and how kind
Ye seemèd by your speech and by your look
The day that ye my hand in bridal took!

"But truly it is said — I know it true,
For at this hour I find it proved on me —
That love grown old is not as when 'twas new;
But certes, lord, for no adversity,
Even to the point of dying, shall it be
That ever I in word or deed repent
That I gave you my heart with full consent.

"My lord, ye know that in my father's cot
Ye had me stripped of all my peasant dress
And richly clad, — ye have not so forgot
The grace ye showed unto my lowliness.
To you I brought but truth, and dispossess
Myself now of your gifts. Here I restore
My robe and wedding ring, forevermore.

"The raiment-chest and jewel-casket both
Are in your chamber, as ye may discern.
Naked from out my father's house," she quoth,
"I came, and naked must I now return;
To do your pleasure is my one concern;
But yet I hope that not in very sense
Of nakedness ye mean to send me hence.

"Ye could not such dishonor do, my lord,
Unto that breast whereon your children lay
As show it bare before the common horde
Of gazers by the road. Wherefore I pray
Not like a worm dispatch me on my way.
Remember, mine own lord, dearer than life,
Unworthy though I was, I was your wife.

"Wherefore in guerdon of the youth I brought,
The youth that hence again I may not bear,
Give me but such a garment, rudely wrought,
As in my girlhood I was wont to wear,
That I therewith may clothe the form of her
Who was your wife, and here I take my leave
Of you, mine own dear lord, lest I you grieve."

"The shift," quoth he, "that thou hast on thy back,
Let it abide and bear it forth with thee."
But force to speak that word did wellnigh lack,
For ruth, this marquis, and away went he.
Before the folk herself disrobèd she,
And in her shift, with head and feet all bare,
Griselda to her father's house doth fare.

The weeping folk attend her on her way,
And Fortune still they curse as they go on,
But she sheds not a tear nor doth she say
A single word, such mastery hath she won
Over herself. Her father, who anon
Heard how his daughter suffered open scorn,
Curses the day and hour when she was born:

Because undoubtedly this poor old man
Had always viewed her marriage with distrust,
For ever through his mind suspicion ran
That when love's shining metal, as it must,
With time and custom should begin to rust,
This lord would think his rank and station high
Shamed by a peasant wife and cast her by.

To meet his daughter hastily he hies,
For by the noise of folk he knew that she
Was near at hand. The teardrops from his eyes
Fell on her, as in her old mantle he
Strove to enfold her, but it might not be,
For that coarse cloak by many a day was now
Older than when she spoke her bridal vow.

Thus with her father, for a certain space,
This perfect flower of wifely patience dwells,
And neither by her words nor in her face,
With few or many, is there aught that tells
A sense of wrong, or spirit that rebels.
Nor seemed she to remember how she sate,
But little while before, in high estate.

No wonder, for, when in her high estate,
Completely humble in her heart was she.
Hers was no pampered palate delicate,
No glistening pomp nor royal vanity;
But full of courteous benignity
She was, discreet and humble, honorable,
And to her husband ever meek and stable.

Men speak of Job, and of his meekness most,
As scholars, when they choose, endite full well;
Especially of men they make their boast,
For little care these clerks to chronicle
The deeds of women; yet, the truth to tell,
No man can be one-half so meek and true
As women are — unless the news is new.

PART VI

Now from Bologna is this great earl come
With his resplendent, stately retinue,
And through the land doth busy Rumor hum
The tidings that he brings with him the new
Marchioness of Salùces, fair to view,
Escorted with such pomp as never eye
Had seen before in all West Lombardy.

The marquis, who had planned the whole event,
The day before this earl was thither come,
Sent for Griselda, that poor innocent,
And with glad visage came she from her home,
But humbly, letting no proud fancies roam;
And reverently falling on her knees,
She waited so to learn what he might please.

"Griselda," quoth this lord, "it is my will,
Unchangeable, that my approaching bride
Be welcomed royally. I would fulfill
All honor so far as my means provide.
And at the feast I would not wound the pride
Of any guest, but each should seated be
And waited on, according to degree.

"I have no women capable, indeed,
Of setting forth my house in fit array,
As I would have it; so in this my need
I bid thee take the charge, as well I may,
For thou hast known my tastes for many a day.
So though thy dress unseemly is and poor,
Do thou thy duty; I demand no more."

"Not only, lord, my duty 'tis," quoth she,
"To do your pleasure, but my heart's desire
To serve you as I may in my degree,
Not fainting though the flesh and spirit tire.
Through weal and woe, through all you may require,
To increase your joy shall be my one endeavor,
As all my love is yours and yours forever."

So saying, she began the house to dight,
To set the tables and the beds to make,
Striving to do the utmost that she might,
Praying the chambermaids for pity's sake
To hurry, sweep, the woven hangings shake,
Whilst she, most serviceable of them all,
Arrayed the bridal rooms and festal hall.

'Twas nigh to noon when did this earl alight,
The earl who with him brought these children twain,
And all the people ran to see the sight,
And marveled at the splendor of the train,
And said to one another it was plain
That Walter was no fool; let bygones rest;
This change of wife, it all was for the best.

For she is fairer, so the folk declare,
Than is Griselda, and of fresher age,
And fairer children and more debonair
Should spring from one of loftier lineage.
The little brother, too, did so engage
Their hearts with winsome looks that, one by one,
They fell to praising what their lord had done.

"O stormy people, sudden and unstable!
Still swayed by what is new, like weather-vane
That with each gust of wind veers on its gable!
For as the moon, now wax ye and now wane;
Still full of tittle-tattle, dear to gain
At half-pence! False your judgment, frail your faith;
Great fool is he that trusts your idle breath."

Thus said the serious people in that city,
When all the populace gazed up and down,
Glad of the novelty, forgetting pity,
Pleased that a new grand lady comes to town.
I say no more of this, for all renown
That I can give is to Griselda due,
So busy all that day, so brave and true.

Full busy was she about everything
Pertaining to the bridal festival,
No wise abashed although her clothes might bring
Disdain upon her, coarse and torn withal;
But with the servants she, queenly and tall,
Went to the gate to greet the marchioness,
Then turned again to duties numberless.

The guests with such blithe welcome she receiveth,
Such courtesy suited to each degree,
No fault is seen in all that she achieveth,
But still men wonder who and what is she
That wears such shabby gown, unfit to see,
But knows all ceremony and all grace,
And they commend her manners and her face.

And she, meanwhile, ceased not this maid to praise
With all her heart, the little lad no less,
So well that no man, though in courtly ways
Well practised, could amend her graciousness;
But when these lords unto the banquet press,
The marquis must unto Griselda call,
As she was busy in the festal hall.

"Griselda," as it were in sport, he saith,
"How likest thou my lady? pleaseth thee?"
"Right well," quoth she, "my lord, for in good faith
I never saw a fairer bride than she.
I pray that God give her prosperity.
Even so I hope that He to you will send
Joyance enough until your lifetime's end.

"But I beseech and warn you of one thing,
That not this maiden, as another, ye
With a continual torment probe and sting,
For she was fostered far more daintily,
And could not suffer such adversity,—
So I suppose — as one like me might bear,
Who had been bred in hardship and in care."

And when this Walter saw her fortitude,
Her smile undimmed, nor bitter words let fall,
And he so often with offenses rude
Had smitten her, still constant as a wall,
So blameless and so beautiful in all,
This marquis, now no longer merciless,
Relented toward her wifely steadfastness.

"This is enough, Griselda mine," quoth he,
"Be now no more sad-hearted nor afraid;
Thy wifely faith and Christian charity,
I have, unto the uttermost, assayed,
Both in thy great estate and ill arrayed.
Thy goodness proved, the rest shall all be bliss,"
And clasped her in his arms with kiss on kiss.

She felt them not, sunk in amazement deep,
Nor heard what he was saying nor replied.
She was as one just startled out of sleep,
Nor woke from her confusion till he cried:
"Griselda, by the Christ that for us died,
Thou art my wife, no other wife I have,
Upon my soul, which God Almighty save.

"This is thy daughter, whom to be my wife
Thou hast supposed; her brother, princely fair,
Thy very son, I promise on my life
Shall be to all the land proclaimed mine heir.
Sent to Bologna, both were nurtured there.
Now take them back; thou can'st not say again
That thou hast nothing of thy children twain.

"And folk that otherwise have said of me,
I tell them I have done this thing I did,
Not out of malice nor of cruelty,
But so to test the virtues in thee hid,
And not to slay my children — God forbid! —
But quietly to have them bred apart,
Till I thy nature knew and all thine heart."

When this she heard, down in a swoon she falleth
For piteous joy, and on reviving she
Both her young children to her softly calleth,
And clasps them in her arms, yet cannot see
Their faces for her tears, but tenderly
Kisseth them o'er and o'er, in mother fashion,
While weeping out her long-repressèd passion.

O what a piteous thing it was to see
Her swooning, and her humble voice to hear!
"Gramercy, lord! I thank you," murmured she,
"For saving me my little children dear.
Now reck I not although I die right here;
Your love and grace assured, whene'er it may
Let my glad soul go forth upon its way.

"O young, O tender, O dear children mine,
Your woeful mother utterly believed
That beasts had eaten you, but your benign,
Good father, and my God who knew how grieved
My heart was, would not have me so bereaved,
But kept you safe," and with that very sound
Of speaking sank she suddenly to ground;

And in her swoon she clasps so firmly still
Her children two, held in a close embrace,
That only with great pains and tender skill
Her clinging arms are loosed. Oh, in that place
Ran many a tear down many a pitying face,
For scarcely could the bystanders behold
That mother's agony so long controlled.

But Walter gladdens her and calms her grief,
And full abashed she riseth from her trance.
All come with blithesome talk to her relief,
Till she again hath caught her countenance.
And sweet it was to see glance answer glance
Between those two, now all estrangement ends,
For like a lover he on her attends.

These ladies, when they saw their time, have drawn
The marchioness into a room with them,
And changed those shabby garments she had on
For cloth of gold, adorned with many a gem,
And crowned her with a jeweled diadem,
And so have led her back into the hall,
Where homage well deserved she had from all.

Thus hath this piteous day a blissful end,
For every man doth all within his might
The hours in mirth and revelry to spend,
Until the welkin shone with starry light,
For far more splendid in all people's sight
This banquet was, and costlier withal,
Than their aforetime marriage festival.

Full many a year in high prosperity
This Walter and Griselda live in rest;
Richly his only daughter married he
Unto a lord, one of the worthiest
Of Italy; and, with all comforts blest,
His wife's old father in his court he keepeth,
Until the soul out of his body creepeth.

His son succeeds to the inheritance
In peace, after his father's day was o'er.
He, too, was happy in his marriage chance,
Though testing not his wife by trials sore.
This world is not so strong as 'twas of yore;
It were not safe to-day such risks to run.
Hearken the moral, now the tale is done.

This story has been told, not that wives should
Follow Griselda in humility,—
It were intolerable though they would—
But so that every wight in his degree
Be even as constant in adversity
As was Griselda. Therefore Petrarch writeth
This story, which in high style he enditeth.

For since a woman in such patience bent
To will of mortal man, far more we ought
To take full cheerfully what God hath sent,
For well may He assay the work He wrought.
And though He tempteth none whom He hath bought
By His own blood, even as Saint James doth say,
He puts us to the trial every day,

And suffereth us, for holy discipline,
With stinging scourges of adversity
To be chastised full oft, but not to win
A knowledge of our hearts, for certes He
Knew all our frailty, ere we came to be;
His government is only for our good;
Then let us live in humble gratitude.

But one word more, good people all, from me:
It were full hard to come on, nowadays,
In a whole town Griseldas two or three;
For now if wives were put to such assays,
This gold that won the Tuscan poet's praise
Is so alloyed with brass, the coin, though fair,
Would break before 'twould bend; so have a care.

Wherefore in honor of the Wife of Bath,
Whose life and all her sect may God maintain
In that high mastery we have heard she hath—
It were a pity else—I'll sing a strain
With merry heart to gladden all this train;
For if my tale were over grave and long,
There's nothing serious about my song.

SONG

Griselda and her patience both are dead,
Buried in Italy. Wherefore I hail
All men so valorous that they have wed
And bid them not their own wives' hearts assail
Nor tempers try, by expectation led
To find Griseldas, for they'll surely fail.

O noble wives, ye dames high-spirited,
Suffer no meek humility to nail
Your noisy tongues; nor let a scholar's head
Spin out for you so marvelous a tale,
Lest ye by that lean cow be swallowèd
Which feeds on patient wives, a diet frail.

Be ye like Echo, not to silence bred,
But ever answering back by hill and dale.
Let no man fool your innocence,—instead,
Be ye the rulers, at your husbands rail.
This lesson should be well rememberèd,
Since to your profit it may much avail.

Ye archwives, strong as camels, stout of tread,
Hit out amain; defend yourselves from bale;
If husbands vex you, let their blood be shed.
And ye, the slender wives, feeble and pale,
Snarl like that cross-grained Indian quadruped,
The tiger; clang like windmill in a gale.

Revere them not and hold them not in dread,
These husbands, for though each be armed in mail,
The arrows of thy crabbèd tongue, well sped,
Shall pierce his armor, be it chain or scale.
Plague him with jealousy and thou shalt see
Him take to cover like a hunted quail.

If thou be fair, then go where feasts are spread;
Display thy face and clothes and quaff good ale.
If thou be ugly, let thy friends be fed
At thine expense, nor be the viands stale.
Ever be light as leaf on linden-tree,
And let thine husband wring his hands and wail.

"Wringing the hands, wailing, and such ado,
I know enough of, eve and morning too,"
The Merchant quoth with bitterness, "and so
Doth many another married man, I trow;

For well I wot it fareth so with me.
I have a wife, the worst that well could be;
For though the very Fiend her husband were,
I swear the Fiend would be no match for her.
Her special faults why need I here review?
For take her all in all, she is a shrew.
Both long and wide the difference between
Griselda's patience and most humble mien
And the surpassing insults of my wife.
Were I once free again, upon my life
I never more would fall into the snare.
We husbands live in sorrow and in care.
Now try it whoso will and to his ruth
He'll find—Saint Thomas help him!—'tis the truth;
That is, in case of most, I say not all;
Nay, God forbid that it should so befall!

"Ah, good Sir Host, who from the Tabard door
Made glad escape, though I've been wed no more
Than these two months, I trow no bachelor,
Though men should stab him to the heart in war,
Could tell so much of agony and fear
As I, were I disposed, could tell you here
About my wife's exceeding viciousness."

"Now," quoth our Host, "Merchant, may God you bless!
But since you understand the wife's black art
So well, I pray you tell to us some part."

"Gladly," quoth he, "but of my private sore,
For sorry heart I may relate no more."

[With this, while slowly sank the weary sun,
That pilgrim of the sky, the Merchant spun
A story of a woman's faithlessness,
Another wife of Lombardy, but less
Remembered than Griselda, nor by me
Shall such a one commemorated be.]

The Merchant

"Eh, mercy on us!" said our Host, all glum,
"Now such a wife I pray God keep me from!
What sleights and subtleties in women meet,
Busy as bees us simple men to cheat!
For they would rather lie than not, alas!
This world is coming to a sorry pass,
As by this Merchant's tale is manifest.
I have a wife — too true — none of the best;
But little was the dower she brought to me,

Yet of her tongue a blabbing shrew is she;
Withal she hath a heap of vices more.
But let it pass! My troubles I forswore
When I set out, yet I'll to you confide
I sore repent that I to her am tied.
But all her faults I dare not tell to you.
'Twould be too risky, it would never do,—
And why? To her 'twould all be told again,
Ay, by a certain gossip in this train,
Whose name I do not need to utter, one
Who tattles all she knows. Nay, I have done.
Besides, my wife's faults are so many, I
Have not the wit to count them, should I try."

[And dodging in and out the Wife of Bath,
Whose vengeful tongue pursued him with her wrath,
Our Host at Ospringe, two score miles and six

Portions of Ancient Hospice on both sides of Water Lane, Ospringe

From London, halted us. A crucifix
Above the door showed us the pilgrim inn,
Where trencher, tankard, pot, and cannikin
Appeased all rancors of the road, and sent
The travelers to their pallets well content.]

THE FOURTH DAY

[Blithe with the morn, we make an early start,
And say our orisons with holy heart,
For only ten miles more the road winds on
Until our journey's end, the shrine, is won.
The silver drops still hanging on the leaves,
Some dewy dream the youthful Squire inweaves
With the fresh time, when poets all rejoice,
But on his musings breaks a burly voice.]

"Squire, come hither, and if your will it be,
Discourse to us of love, for certes ye
Know of that art as much as any man."

"Nay, nay, good sir," quoth he, "but as I can
I'll do my part, for I would not rebel
Against your rule. A story will I tell.
Hold me excusèd, if I speak amiss.
My will is good, and lo, my tale is this."

THE SQUIRE'S TALE

At Sarra, in the land of Tartary,
There dwelt a king, and with the Russ[1] warred he,
Through which there perished many a doughty man.—
This noble king by name was Cambuscán,
And in his time was of so great renown,
That nowhere else there sat beneath a crown
So excellent a lord in everything.

[1] The Russian.

Him lacked there nought belonging to a king,
Within the creed to which his race was born.
He kept the law to which he had been sworn;
And thereto he was hardy, rich, and wise,
Always the same, serene of soul and eyes,
Piteous and just, benign and honorable,

The Squire

Of his brave heart as any center stable;
Young, fresh, and strong, in arms desirous,
As any bachelor of all his house.
A fair person he was, and fortunate;
And always kept so well a king's estate,
That there was nowhere such another man.

This noble king, this Tartar, Cambuscán,
Two princes had by Elfeta his wife,
Of which the eldest was named Algarsife,
The other Cambalo: and there was born
Also a daughter to him, like the morn,
Younger than both, whose name was Canace:
But to relate how beautiful was she,
Passeth the reach of my poetic wing;
I dare not undertake so high a thing.
Mine English too sufficeth not. A man
Had need an Ovid be, or Mantuan,
And know all colors fitted for the art,
To show you what she was, in the least part;
I am none such. Plain speech must be my plan.
And so befell that when this Cambuscán
Had twenty winters been a crownèd king,
He bade, as was his custom in the spring,
The feast of his nativity be cried
In Sarra, his great city, far and wide,
The news whereof was glad to every ear.

Phoebus, the sun, full jovial was, and clear;
For he was mounting nigh his exaltation
In Mars's face, and in his house and station
In Aries, the choleric hot sign.[1]
Full lusty was the weather, and benign;
For which the birds, against the sunny sheen,
What for the season and the sprouting green,
Securely and full loud sang their affections:
They seemed to say,—We now have got protections
Against the sword of winter, keen and cold.

[1] The astrological way of saying it was the middle of March.

This royal king then, glorious to behold
With crown and ermine, sat upon his dais
In his great hall, in all the people's gaze,
And held his feast, so rich and so serene,
In all the world was no such other seen.
What need describe it? for to tell the array,
And half the meats, would take a summer's day;
And therefore I pass by their dainty shows,
Their swans, and peacocks, and their heronneaus,[1]
With meats that by a Tartar seneschal
Are held full dear, though here we count them small.
Besides, the bell hath warned me it is prime,[2]
And I must trespass not on others' time,
But into closer strain my theme enforce.

And so befell, that after the third course,
While that this king sat thus in his array,
Hearing his minstrels and his harpers play
Before him at his board deliciously,
In at the hall door, lo! all suddenly
There came a knight upon a steed of brass,
That in his hand a mirror held of glass;
Upon his thumb he had a golden ring,
And by his side a naked sword hanging;
And up he rideth to the royal board.
In all the hall there was not spoke a word
For marvel of this knight. Him to behold
Full busily they waited, young and old.

This strange knight, that appeared thus suddenly,
All armed except his head, full gorgeously,
Saluteth king and queen, and nobles all,

---

[1] Young herons.
[2] Nine o'clock.

In order as they sat within the hall,
With so high reverence and regardfulness,
Both in his word and in his whole address,
That Gawain's self, with his old courtesy,[1]
Had he left Fairyland, and stood thereby,
Had not improved him in a single thing:
And after this, strait looking at the king,
His message with a manly voice he spoke,
After the form belonging to his folk,
With not a fault of syllable or letter;
And that his meaning might be felt the better,
His cheer was suited to his words; as teach
Those learnèd wits, that ken the art of speech.
I may not tell it as he did: my strain
Is far too weak such rhetoric to attain.
Yet to repeat it, in a common way,
As showing what at large he meant to say,
Thus much will I attempt to call to mind:

"My lord, the king of Araby and Inde,
My sovereign master, on this solemn day,
Saluteth you, as he best can and may,
And sendeth you, in honor of your feast,
By me, your ready servant though your least,
This steed of brass; which well, as in this hall,
Can, in the space of a day natural,
That is to say, in four and twenty hours,
Where'er you list, in sunshine or in showers,
Carry your body into every place,
In which it please you show your sovereign face,
Nor stain you with a speck, through foul or fair;
Or if you list to sail as high in air

1 Sir Gawain, that Knight of the Round Table most renowned for courtesy.

As doth an eagle, when he wills to soar,
This same good steed shall bear you evermore
Without a peril (though ye take no keep
Of bridle as ye go; nay, sit and sleep);
Then turn again with writhing of a pin.
He, sir, that made it, knew all arts herein,
And waited upon many a constellation
While patiently he worked his operation,
And knew full many a seal, and many a bond.[1]

"This glass I hold, clear as a diamond,
Hath such a power, that in it men may see
When there shall happen any adversity
Unto your reign, or to yourself; and know,
By very sight, who is your friend or foe:
And more than this, if any lady bright
Have set her heart on any thankless knight,
And he be false, here shall the lady see
His new love, and his thorough subtlety,
So plain and clear, that nothing he shall hide.

"Wherefore against this lusty summer-tide,
This glass, and this ring also, my lord, he
Hath sent unto my lady Canace,
Your excellent daughter that is here;—a thing
So virtuous, this simple-seeming ring,
That let her bear it, either on her hand,
Or in her purse, and she will understand
The tongue and speech of every fowl that flies,
And answer him in his own birdly wise.
Also each herb that groweth shall she read,

[1] It was made by a magician at a time when the stars were favorable.

And whom it may avail, though that he bleed
From dreadful wounds, never so deep and wide.

"This naked sword, that hangeth by my side,
Such virtue hath, that whomsoe'er it smite,
Clean through his armor will it carve and bite,
Were it as thick as is a branchêd oak;
And whosoe'er is wounded with the stroke,
Shall never be whole man, till of your grace
It please you stroke him in the wounded place
With the flat side. The wound will then be closed.
All this is truth, sir. Nothing have I glosed.
Nor while 'tis held in hand, will the sword fail."

And when the stranger thus hath told his tale,
He backeth from the hall with reverent heed,
And so, forth issuing, lighteth from the steed.
The steed, which like the sun for brightness
 shone,
Stood in the court as still as any stone.
The knight hath doffed his armor for a vest
Of peace, and sitteth as an honored guest;
And to a tower, where all high gifts are stored,
Are borne in state the mirror and the sword.
But unto Canace is borne the ring,
Solemnly, there as she sat next the king.
As to the horse, immovable it stood,
Stuck to the ground, as though it had been glued:
Nor had it stirred, I ween, though folk had brought
Pulley or windlass. It had served them nought.
And why? Because none knew the mystery;
And so they left him, standing steadfastly,

Till, sometime before dusk, the knight may choose
To show them how to stir his brazen thews.

Great was the press came swarming to and fro
To gaze upon this steed, that standeth so;
For it was of a make so broad, and long,
And high, and so proportioned to be strong,
It matched therein a steed of Lombardy,
And yet withal it was so quick of eye,
So "horsely," and so full of airy grace,
It might have been of gentle Apulian race.
The people thought so; and were all agreed,
From tail to ear it was a matchless steed.
But what incessantly amazed them, was
How it could go like life, and yet was brass:
All deemed it a thing magical; but then
How made, and by what sort of man of men?
Divers the folk, divers the fantasy:
For just as many wits as heads there be.
They murmured like a swarm, out of the hive:
Some deemed the creature senseless, some alive;
Some likened it, from what is told to us
By the old poets, to the Pegasus,—
The horse that had the wings; and others feared
It might be like the Greek horse, that appeared
Within Troy town, and laid the city low.
Quoth one of these,—"I dread it: for I trow
Soldiers are stuffed therein, and 'tis a plot.
'Twere well the thing were looked into, God wot."
Another whispered, "He's a fool, this clerk;
'Tis manifestly some magician's work;
Some juggle, sirs; a kind of—sort of—trick:"

And others doubt, whether some heretic
Might not have wrought it, or some infidel,
And whether, taking it, the king did well.
For what mean spirits may not comprehend,
They gladly construe to the baser end.

Some again marveled on the glass, and how
Fools could suppose it what they heard but now.
But others said, it might be well supposed,
Since natural art found wondrous things enclosed
In angles and reflections, as a pond
Encloseth scenes beside it, and beyond:
In Rome, they said, was such a glass; and, lo!
Read what Alhazen[1] and Vitellio,[2]
And other wits have spoken in their lives,
That writ of mirrors and of perspectives,
As Aristotle did to please his lord.

Others again marveled upon the sword,
That pierced through everything; and fell in speech
Of Telephus, whose wound, instead of leech,
Was by the quaint spear of Achilles closed,
Right in such wise as hath been just supposed.
Of metals, and of medicines therewithal,
And from their compounds what strange things
might fall,
Much they discoursed; but more than I may tell;
And then upon the lady's ring they fell
And said they never heard of craft so strange,
Save what by some was deemed within the range
Of Moses's wisdom, and of Solomon's;
And then they spake apart, in lower tones.

1 An Arabian astronomer of the eleventh century.
2 A Polish astronomer of the thirteenth century.

Nevertheless, some argued, strange it was
To see fern-ashes made a cause of glass,
Since glass in nought resembleth ash of fern;
Only in thus far reaching to discern
The cause of glass, men leave to stare and wonder.
So happeth it in wond'ring upon thunder,
On ebb and flood, on gossamer and mist,
And all things else, until the cause is wist.
Thus jangle they, and reason, and devise,
Till that the king 'gan from his board arise.

Phoebus hath left his chair meridional,
And now was moving towards the Lion's stall,
(The gentle beast, with his star Aldrian)[1]
When that this Tartar king, this Cambuscán,
Rose from his board, there as he sat full high:
Before him goeth the loud minstrelsy;
And thus he paceth to his painted hall,
Where other music soundeth over all,
And played such things, it was a heaven to hear.

And now went lusty Venus' children dear
Dancing away; for in the Fish full high
She sat, and viewed them with a friendly eye.[2]

This noble king is set upon his throne;
The stranger knight is brought to him anon,
And goeth down the dance with Canace.

Here rageth now the sport and jollity,
Such as no dull man fitteth to devise:
He must have known Love well and his bright eyes,
And been a festive soul, as fresh as May,

[1] The astrological way of saying that it was nearly two o'clock.
[2] That is, the planet Venus being in favorable position, lovers are mirthful, — the knights and ladies are disposed to dance.

To dare to hope to tell you the array.
Who else could speak of all the forms of dances
Dulcet and wild, and the fresh countenances
Full of such looks and such dissimulings,
For fear of jealous men's discoverings?
No man but Launcelot, and he is dead.
Therefore I pass by all this lustyhead,
And say no more; leaving, in midst of all,
The mirth to spin, till men to supper call.

The steward bade the spicers haste, and see
The wines made hot, during this melody;
And now the ushers and the squires are gone;
The spicers and the butlers come anon;
They eat and drink, and when this hath an end,
The company unto the temple wend,
As reason is; and then they sup by day.
What need instruct you of this new array?
Who wotteth not, that at a prince's feast
Is plenty for the greatest and the least,
And dainties more than such as I may know?

So after supper this great king must go
To see the horse of brass, with all a rout
Of ladies and of lords him round about;
For such a wond'ring was there on this thing,
That since the siege of Troy, which poets sing,
Where on a horse was wond'ring among men,
Never was such a wond'ring as was then.
But, finally, the king asketh the knight
The virtue of this courser, and the might,
And prayed him to detail his governance.

This horse anon began to trip and dance,
Soon as the knight laid hand upon the rein,
Who said, "There is no more, sir, to explain
Or bear in mind when we two speak alone,
Than trill a pin here, as shall then be shown;
Yet also you must name your journey's end:
Likewise must bid him, when you please, descend,
Then trill another pin, and then will he
Go down where'er you please full easily,
And rest, whate'er betide him, in one spot,
Though all the world be sworn that he shall not.
Trill yet this other pin, and in a wink
Vanish will he, whither no soul may think
And yet return, be it by day or night,
The moment he is called, as swift as light.
Ride where you list, there's no more need be done."

When thus the king his lesson had begun,
And furthermore, when, whispering with the knight,
He knew the thing and its whole form aright,
Full glad was he; then turning with his train
Repaired him to his mirth yet once again.
The bridle to a tower is borne, and there
Laid up among the jewels, rich and rare;
The horse has vanished, I may not tell how;
And I myself, awhile, must vanish now,
Leaving this Cambuscán, this noble king,
Feasting his lords till day was nigh to spring.

PART II

The nourisher of good digestion, sleep,
'Gan on them wink, and bade their thoughts take keep

That mirth as well as labor will have rest;
And with a gaping mouth, the king expressed
The will of Sleep, that it was time for bed,
For blood was dominant in drowsy head.[1]
"Cherish the friend of nature, blood," quoth he.
Gaping, they gave him thanks, by two and three,
And so the company withdrew to rest,
As Sleep so willed. They took it for the best.

The dreams they dreamt shall not be told for me.
Full were their heads of feast's fumosity,
Which causeth men, without a horse, to fly.
They slept, until the day was broad and high,
The most of them,—save lady Canace;
For like sweet maiden, temperate was she,
And of her father had she taken leave,
To go to rest, soon after it was eve;
She wished not to look pale next day, nor be
In aught unfitting the festivity.
And so she slept her first sleep, and then woke;
For such a pleasure in her heart she took
Of her two presents by the stranger brought,
She twenty times changed color at the thought.
Now for the ring, now for the glass it was;
And in a dream she saw things in the glass.
Wherefore, before the sun 'gan up to glide,
She called the good dame sleeping by her side,
And said it was her pleasure to arise.
The good old dame, that was as gladly wise
As her sweet self (in sooth had trained her so),
Said smilingly, "Why, where then would ye go?
For all the people, Madam, are in bed."

1 Old physicians taught that the physical element, "the blood," has rule over man from 8 p. m. to 3 a. m.

"I cannot sleep, do all I may," she said;
"And so I would arise and walk about."

This good old lady calleth the whole rout
Of women, and they rise, and bustleth she,
And riseth also then fresh Canace,
As ruddy and bright as is the vernal sun,
When in the Ram his fourth degree is run;
No higher was he when he viewed her face;[1]
And forth she walketh at an easy pace,
Arrayed, as suiteth with the lusty prime,
Lightly to play, and to enjoy the time
With some few maidens of her company;
And forth into the park thus moveth she.

The vapor, breathing upward on her road,
Maketh the sun to seem ruddy and broad.
Nathless the dawning was so fair a sight,
It made the hearts in all their bosoms light;
And she herself, what for the time of day,
And the sweet birds, and all she heard them
say,
By reason of the ring, halteth full oft,
And listeneth, and laugheth, glad and soft.

The one main point, whenever tale is told,
If it be tarried, till the ear grow cold,
Loseth its savor, whatsoe'er it be,
For fulsomeness of the prolixity;
Wherefore her walking getteth no more
words;
I come at once, so please ye, to the birds.

1 That is at sunrise on March sixteenth.

Amidst a tree all dry, as white as chalk,
As Canace was playing in her walk,
There sat a falcon over head, full high,
That with a piteous voice so 'gan to cry,
And beat herself so hard with both her wings,
That all the wood rang with her sufferings,
And the red blood went trickling down the tree;
And ever shrieked and flapped herself thus she,
And with her beak so tore into her breast,
That never was brute beast, the cruellest,
That had not wept (if beasts could weep) to hear
How loud she shrieked. It was a very fear.

Now never lived the fowler that could tell
Of falcons, and describe their beauty well,
Who spoke of one which might with this compare
For gentle shape as well as plumage fair.
She seemed a Falcon Peregrine,[1] far flown;
And ever and anon she gave a groan
For lack of blood, and in a swoon went she,
Till she had well nigh fallen from the tree.

This fair king's daughter, Canace, whose ring
Upon her finger told her every thing
Which birds might say, or might be said to birds,
Hath comprehended all the falcon's words;
And to the tree she hasteth fearfully,
And at the bird uplooketh piteously,
And holdeth her lap wide to save her fall,
In case again she swoon on the tree tall:
And a long while so stood and waited she,
Till at the last she spoke full tenderly:—

1 A Pilgrim Falcon, away from her nest.

"What is the cause," quoth she, "if ye may tell,
That thus ye be in very pain of hell?
Take heed; I pray thee, groveling there above:
Is it for grief of death, or loss of love?
For these are the two things that cause most woe
In gentle heart. Nought else could grieve thee so.
Yourself ye wreak upon yourself; which showeth,
No other cause of your sharp deed there goeth,
Nor do I see ye chased by other creature.
For love of God, and as ye are of nature
Gentle and free, say what may help ye best;
For never saw I yet, from east to west,
Creature that fared with its own self so ill:
Truly, ye slay me with your woeful will.
Come down, for God's sake, from the tree; do, bird;
And on the faith of a king's daughter's word,
I will amend your sorrow, if I may,
With all my might, and that ere close of day,
So help me the great God that made us all.
As for your wounds, here's hyssop on the wall,
And balm, and myrrh, shall swiftly salve that trouble."

But at these words the falcon 'gan redouble
Her piteous shrieks, till with a heavy groan
She fell to earth, and lay there as a stone.
As lieth a still stone, so lieth she.
Canace, in her lap full tenderly,
Taketh her up, and from her swoon she waketh,
And when delivered from her swoon she breaketh
Her silence into words, and thus hath spoken:—

"That gentle heart hath pity on heart broken
May well be thought, since any small distress
Winneth such heart to show its gentleness.
I know thou pitiest me, fair Canace,
Of very womanly benignity
Which Nature in your loving heart hath set.
And yet, out of no hope to break my net,
But to obey a heart so kind and free,
And to warn others by unhappy me,
As the great lion by the whelp was taught,
Right for such cause, and in no other thought,
While I yet breathe, and can speak leisurely,
This heart, now breaking, will I show to thee."

While thus the bird was speaking, the king's daughter
Wept, as if she were turning into water,
Till that the falcon bade her to be still,
And with a sigh obeyed her gentle will.

"Well was I born," quoth she; "alas the day!
And fostered in a rock of marble gray
So tenderly, that nothing ailed me long:
I knew not what misfortune was, nor wrong,
Till I could flee, under the heavens, full high.

"There dwelt a tiercelet[1] in the place, hard by,
Who seemed a well of very crystal truth,
All were he deep in every fault of youth.
He wrapped it all so close in humble cheer,
And had a way so purely sweet and clear,
And was so pleasant, and so busy kind,
No traitor could have guessed his traitorous mind;—

[1] Hawk.

Full deep in grain he dyed his pleasing powers;—
Yea, as the serpent hideth under flowers
Till such time as the bite proclaimeth it,
Right so this God of Love's own hypocrite
Put forth all sweets that make the shows of love:—
And as on tombstone all is fair above,
But under is the corpse, such as ye wot,
Such was this hypocrite, so fair, yet not;
And in this wise he fashioned his intent,
That, save the Fiend, none dreamed of what he meant,
And served, and wept, and plained, and spoke of death,
Till that my heart, too soft beneath such breath,
Gave him its love, in very thanks for his,
Not knowing how enough to pay such bliss.
And when he found his triumph gone so far,
And that my star had bowed beneath his star,
He cared no more, although no more he won,
But left me, with a foolish heart undone,
And set his wits to gain as much elsewhere,
This being all his love, and all his care.

"Lord! with what cunning he would feign delight,
With what sweet reverence and subjected might!
How rapt, yet not beyond respect, for joy!
That never Jason, nor the star of Troy,[1]
Jason!—no certes, nor since Lamlech's age
That first loved two,[2] no man on earth could wage
Such magic war, the twenty thousandth part,
With the poor outworks of a loving heart.
His happy manner was a heaven to see
To any woman; and so charmed it me,
And I so loved him, and so watched his eyes,

[1] Paris, who deserted Oenoné for Helen, as Jason deserted Medea for Glaucé.
[2] Adah and Zillah.

For any look that might therein arise,
That did he suffer, the least bit on earth,
Fell there a speck of shadow on his mirth,
A pang so keen into my breast would shoot,
Methought I felt death twisting mine heart's root.

"He went, alas! and one thing dare say I,
I know what I but thought I knew, thereby;
I know what is the pain of death indeed.
You might have sworn you saw his own heart bleed
When that he went, his look was so like mine,
So sorrowful; but it was all design.
He said his honor willed that he must go,
And I so thought, since oft it falleth so.
I made a virtue of necessity,
And held my hand out, since 'twas so to be,
And took his own, and hid from him my grief,
Well as I could, to give his heart relief,
And said,—'Lo! I am yours, and shall be, ever.'
I am. But him I shall see more, no, never.

"What answered he, it needeth not rehearse:
Who can say better things? who can do worse?
I trow he had the ancient text in mind,
Which saith, that all things, pairing with their kind,
Gladden their hearts. Thus argue men, I guess;
And what men pair with, is newfangleness;
They act, as birds do, which they feed in cages:
For though they, day and night, tend them like pages,
And strew the bird's room fair and soft as silk,
And give him sugar, honey, bread, and milk,
Yet right anon, let but his door be up,

And with his feet he spurneth down his cup,
And to the wood will he, and feed on worms.—
In that new college keepeth he his terms,
And learneth love of his own proper kind;
No gentleness of home his heart may bind.

"So fared it with this tiercelet, woe's the day!
Though he were gently born, and fresh, and
gay,
And goodly to behold, and humble and free,
Yet on a time he saw a new bird flee,
And suddenly he loved this new bird so,
That from his falcon must his fancy go,
And he be hers, and look no more on me;
Alas! alas! and there's no remedy,
Nor death itself, methinks, will let me die."

And with that word this falcon 'gan to cry,
And swooneth oft within the lady's lap.
Great was the sorrow made for her mishap
By Canace and by her maidens all:
They knew not how their help might best befall;
Yet Canace home beareth in her lap
The wounded thing, and hasteth to enwrap
The part in balsams, which the beak had hurt.
Then dug she in the ground for plant and wort
Of precious kinds; and day and night she drew
Sanatives thence; and by her bed a mew[1]
All soft she set, with azure velvet lined,
To show the truth[2] that is in womankind;
But all without she had it painted green,
On which all false and mankind fowls were seen;

[1] Cage.
[2] "True blue."

And pies and daws coming on every side
With open mouths, to spite them and to chide.

Thus leave I Canace to keep her bird:—
Of her ring now I speak no other word,
Nor shall, till in good time my theme explain
How that this falcon gat her love again,
Repentant, as the Tartar stories show,
By mediation of Prince Cambalo,
Son of the king, as at the first was told.
Meantime through fields of battle must I hold
My purposed way, and such adventures tell,
As never in the world the like befell.

First will I tell of this great Cambuscán,
That in his time full many a city wan;
And after will I speak of Algarsife,
How that he won Theodora to his wife,
For whom full oft in peril great he was,
Had help not reached him in the horse of brass;
And after will I speak of Cambalo,
That fought in tourney with the brethren two,
Ere that the victor might his sister win;[1]
And where I left, there will I fresh begin.

[And here our Poet left the tale half-told,
Or some few leaves were lost from out his fold
Of precious manuscript ere with hushed tread
There sought the chamber of the Master dead
Reverent disciples who for unborn men
Traced and retraced the labors of his pen;
For wellnigh four score years were yet to be

1 This part of the story was taken up by Spenser in his "Faerie Queene," iv, 3.

Before a greater marvel, verily,
Than Cambuscán's keen sword or horse of brass,
Than Canace's quaint ring or magic glass,
Should come to us from fairyland — no less
A miracle than Caxton's printing-press.]

"In faith, young Squire, thou hast thee well acquitted,
Like one of gentle blood and ready-witted,'
The Franklin quoth. "Considering thy youth,
So feelingly thou speakest, sir, in sooth,
That in my judgment there is no one here
That shall be counted, if thou live, thy peer
In eloquence. God give thee happy chance
And in thy virtues fair continuance!
For great delight thy words have given me.
I have a son and, by the Trinity,
Rather than worth of twenty pound in land,
Though were the deed right now within my hand,
I would he were so promising as thou.
Fie on possessions! would one might endow
An heir with character and heart and brain!
Oft have I chid my son and shall again,
For he sets naught by virtue and discretion,
But all that he may have in his possession
He stakes at dice and loses. He cares more
To chat with pages at a palace door
Than enter in and hear of deeds of daring
And learn from gentlefolk a gentle bearing."

"Straw for your 'gentle bearing'!" quoth our Host.
"What, Franklin! Marry, sir! right well thou know'st

That by our compact every man of you
Who keeps his word must tell a tale or two."

"That know I well, sir," courteously quoth he.
"I pray you, treat me not disdainfully,
Though with this Squire I talked a minute so."

"Tell on thy tale, and let thy talking go."

The Franklin

"Gladly, Sir Host," quoth he, "I will obey
Your sovereign will; now hearken what I say.
I would not thwart you, not in any wise,
So far as my abilities suffice.
I hope my tale may not bring down rebuff
On me again. I call it good enough.

"These gentle Bretons, in their bygone days,
Of strange adventures made them many lays,
Renownèd in the early Breton tongue,
Lays that to divers instruments they sung,
Or else read them aloud for social pleasure,
And one of these in memory I treasure,
Which I'll relate to you as best I can.

"But, sirs, because I'm an unlettered man,
Even at the outset do I you beseech,
Hold me excusèd for my homespun speech;
For rhetoric was never taught to me,
And bare and plain must all my language be.
Upon Parnassus Mount I never slept,
Like Cicero, nor am I an adept
In figurative speech,—'colors', they say,
'Of style'. But all the colors that I may
Distinguish are those blooming in the meadow
Or such as painters with their brushes shadow.
Colors of language are too curious
For my perception; but my tale runs thus:"

[The Franklin's story proved his knowledge of
A better lore than rhetoric, as love,
Of which this very subtlety he told:
"Love will not be by mastery controlled.
When mastery cometh, the God of Love, anon,
Beateth his wings, and farewell, he is gone.
Love is a thing as any spirit free."
Also of truth an echoing word spake he:
"Truth is the highest thing a man may keep."
Well showed the tale how noble deed shall reap

A noble harvest; let man generous be,
And lo! the sleeping generosity
In other men wakens to meet his own.
After the Franklin, spake in softer tone
The Second Nun and told the holy life
Of Saint Cecilia, lily-hearted wife,
Who wears the palm of martyrdom in bliss;
And full devoutly did we hearken this.]

The Second Nun

When told was Saint Cecilia's life, ere we
Had ridden five miles from our hostelry,

A rider overtook us, one who had
Black outer-garments and beneath was clad
In a white surplice; such was his array.
The nag he rode, which was all dapple gray,
So sweated it was wonderful to see.
He must have spurred three miles. With him had he
A Yeoman, whose horse, too, was sweating so
That scarcely might the weary creature go.
Foam stood about the breastplate; in effect,
He as a magpie was with foam all flecked.
A wallet doubled on his crupper lay;
He seemed to carry little fine array.
Light-clad for summer rode this worthy man,
And in mine heart to wonder I began
Who might he be, till I espied his hood
Was fastened to his cloak and understood,
After a long deliberation, he
Some sort of Canon, or the like, might be.
Way down his back his hat hung by a string,
For his was more than common galloping;
The man had spurred like mad. Beneath his hood
He had a burdock leaf to cool his blood,
And guard his head, with perspiration wet.
It was a joy to see that Canon sweat.
His forehead there was dripping like a still
All full of herbs. He called us sharp and shrill,
As he came up by dint of spur and whip.
"God save," quoth he, "this merry fellowship!
Fast have I pricked, good people, for your sake,
Because I longed your troop to overtake
And ride in such a jocund company."
His Yeoman, too, was full of courtesy

And said: "Fair sirs, this very morningtide
Out of your hostelry I saw you ride,
And warned my lord and master sovereign,
Who to ride with you is exceeding fain,
For well he loveth sport and dalliance."

"God for thy warning send thee happy chance,
Good friend!" replied our Host, "for it would seem
Thy lord were wise and so I well may deem.
But blithe he is as well, I warrant you.
Can he perchance tell us a tale or two,
Wherewith to gladden all this company?"

"Who, sir? my lord? yea, yea, and that can he.
He knows of jollity and merriment
Enough, sir, any party to content.
If ye knew him as well as I do, then
Ye would count him a marvel among men,
So well and craftily, in sundry wise,
His wit can work. For many an enterprise,
Great things, full hard for any here to do
Without his helping, he has carried through.
Though in such homely guise with you he rideth,
'Tis luck for all in whom my lord confideth.
If ye but knew him, ye were blest, I trow;
Not for great riches would ye then forego
His fellowship. All that I have I'll stake
On his discretion. Ye my word may take,—
My master is a very paragon."

"Well!" quoth our Host, "prithee, good friend, ride on
Awhile with me. Is he a man of lore?"

"Nay," quoth the Yeoman, "this my lord is more
Than scholar, and I'll briefly tell to you
A little of the wonders he can do.

The Canon's Yeoman

"I say, my master hath such magic power—
I know not all of it, yet many an hour
I've worked by his instruction and his chiding—
That all this ground on which we now are riding,

Until we come to Canterbury town,
He could, I say, clean turn it upside down,
And pave it all with silver and with gold.''

And when the Yeoman had this story told
Unto our Host, he said: "Now bless my
heart!
This thing is passing strange that ye impart.
Since this thy lord hath judgment nothing dim,
Judgment for which men ought to honor him,
Why doth his worship weigh himself so light?
That cloak of his it is not worth a mite,
Not for so great a person, I'll be sworn;
It is all soiled; besides, 'tis somewhat torn.
Why is thy lord so sluttish when he can
Buy better raiment, if he is the man
Thy words declare him? Prithee, tell me that.
Out with it. No one overhears our chat."

"Why do ye ask?" this Yeoman quoth. "In
sooth
He'll never prosper. But though this be truth,
I'll not stand by it. Keep it secret, pray.
I think he is too wise to make his way.
Food that is overdone is never nice;
Excess of virtue, scholars say, is vice.
'Tis just in this I hold he misses it;
For when a man hath over-great a wit,
'Tis too unwieldy for this world's affairs,
And oft it fails him, taken unawares.
My master's case is such, it grieves me sore;
God it amend! I must not tell you more."

"Never mind that, good Yeoman," quoth our Host.
"Since of the cunning of thy lord thou know'st,
Tell how he works, I pray, this wizard sly.
His craft, his mystery, how doth he ply?
Where do ye dwell, if that may spoken be?"

"Out in the suburbs of a town," quoth he,
"Lurking in corners and blind lanes, where thieves
And highwaymen and all that to them cleaves
Take up their secret fearful residence,
As men that dare not, for some foul offense,
Walk openly. Even so, in sooth, fare we."

"Now," quoth our Host, "still let me talk to thee.
Why art thou so discolored of thy face?"

"Peter!" quoth he. "God give it sorry grace
I am so used my master's fire to blow,
I may have altered my complexion so.
Not in a mirror 'tis my wont to pry,
But sore I toil and learn to 'multiply',—
This is the art, in private be it told,
Of turning baser metals into gold.
All mazed we grow with poring o'er the fire,
Yet for all that we fail of our desire,
For always do we miss the end in view.
Deluded folk lend us a pound or two,
Or more, for we assure them we have found
A certain way of doubling every pound,—
So much, at very least, while none can tell
The end of wealth within the crucible.
Yet is it false, but still we have good hope,

That we may do it: after it we grope;
But still that art so far beyond us lies
We may not overtake it, for it hies
Away so quickly, flits from us so fast,
'Twill make us beggars, that it will, at last."

While thus the Yeoman let their secrets fall,
The alchemist stole up and heard it all,
For still this Canon was uneasy when
He noted private conference of men,
For Cato says the guilty still doth deem
He is of every whispering the theme.
And that was why the Canon drew so near
His Yeoman, that he might thus overhear
What he was saying. Cried he, when he heard:

"Hold thou thy peace. Speak not another word,
For if thou do, that word shall cost thee dear.
Thou slanderest me in this assemblage here
And tellest matters thou art bound to hide."

"So?" quoth our Host. "Tell on, whate'er betide.
Of all his threatening reck thou not a mite."

"In faith," the Yeoman said, "I hold it light."

And when this Canon saw it so would be,
That this his man would tell his privacy,
He fled away for sorrow and for shame.

"Ha!" quoth the Yeoman. "Now we'll play the game.
All that I know I'll tell you right anon,
Since he — the foul Fiend grapple him! — is gone.
For never more shall I with him be found,

I promise you, for penny nor for pound.
Who first led me this calling to embrace,
Sorrow and shame be his! My smoke-stained face
Proves that to me 'twas earnest, by my faith.
That feel I well, whatever any saith.
And yet for all my smarts, my stinging eyes,
My toil and peril, not in any wise
Could I that tempting, cursèd furnace quit.
Now would to God I had sufficient wit
To tell you all the secrets of that art,
But ne'ertheless I will reveal a part;
Since now my lord is gone, I will not spare
All that I know, so please you, to declare."

[Then told the Yeoman of the tricks there be
Within this "sliding science," alchemy,
This "elfish craft" that lives by lie and cheat;
Yet have these alchemists such bitter-sweet
Hope for the morrow's trial, though to-day's
Has failed, that still they move as in a maze,
Spending their all to find that they have got
Naught for their labors but a broken pot.]

Now wot ye not where stands a little town
Which thereabouts they call Bob-up-and-down,
Under the Blee,[1] in Canterbury way?
Well, there our Host began to jest and play,
And said, "Oho now! Dun is in the mire.[2]
What, sirs, will nobody, for prayer or hire,
Waken our fellow dropt so far behind?
Here were a bundle for a thief to find.
See, how he noddeth! by St. Peter, see!

1 Blean Forest, where pilgrims went in fear of thieves.
2 The cry in an old game of log-lifting, equivalent to "The horse is stuck."

He'll tumble off his saddle presently.
Is that a Cook of London? Mischief take him!
Bring him up to pay his forfeit. Wake him, wake him!
We'll have his tale to keep him from his nap,
Although the drink turn out not worth the tap.

The Black Prince's Well, Harbledown

Awake, thou Cook," quoth he; "God give thee woe!
What aileth thee to sleep by daylight so?
Did Ospringe fleas the God of Slumber bite?
Or did'st thou swill the pilgrim ale all night,
So thou can'st not hold up thy drunken head?"

This Cook, that was full pale and nothing red,
Stared up and said unto our Host: "God bless
My soul! There weighs on me such heaviness,
I know not why, that I would rather sleep
Than drink of the best gallon-wine in Cheap"[1]

The Manciple

"Well," quoth the Manciple, "if it might ease
Thine head, Sir Cook, and also none displease

[1] The main thoroughfare in old London.

Of all here riding in this company,
And mine Host grant it, I would pass thee by,
Till thou art better, and so tell my tale;
For in good faith thy visage is full pale;
Thine eyes grow dull, methinks; and sure I am
Thy breath resembleth not sweet marjoram,
Which showeth thou can'st utter no good matter:
Nay, thou may'st frown, forsooth, but I'll not flatter.
See, how he gapeth, lo! this boozy-brain,
As he would swallow up the pilgrim train.
Hold close thy mouth, man, by thy father's kin;
Now may the Devil set his foot therein
And stop it up, for 'twill infect us all;
Fie, what a pigsty! foul thy grunt befall!
Look out! he's reeling! there, sirs, was a swing!
Take care! he's bent on tilting at the ring:
He's the shape—isn't he?—to tilt and ride!
Avaunt, you swine! go to your straw and hide."

Now with these words the Cook waxed wroth, and fast
He nodded on the Manciple, for past
Speaking he was, and from his horse fell he,
And where he fell, there lay he patiently,
Till pity on his shame his fellows took.
Here was a pretty horseman of a Cook!
Alas! that he had held not by his ladle!
And ere again they got him on his saddle,
There was a mighty shoving to and fro
To lift him up, and muckle care and woe,
So unwieldy was this sorry, pallid ghost.
Then to the Manciple thus spake our Host:—
"Since drink upon this man hath domination,

Sir, by the hope I have of my salvation,
I trow he would have told but ill his tale;
For whether it be wine, or it be ale,
That he hath drunk, he speaketh through the nose,
And sneezeth thick and fast, as when there grows
A cold in head. Besides, we have enow
To do in keeping him out of the slough,
And if he tumble from his horse again,
Another weary hour 'twill cost us then
To heave that heavy, drunken body up,
Tell on thy tale; his left he in the cup.
But, Manciple, thou yet may'st pay a price
For taunting him so roundly with his vice.
Perchance some day he'll do as much for thee,
And bid the lawyers, whom thou feedest, see
How well thy reckonings square. That were a trick,
To set them conning thine arithmetic."

"Mine," quoth the Manciple, "were then the mire!
Much rather would I pay his horse's hire,
And that will be no trifle, mud and all,
Than risk the peril of so sharp a fall.
I did but jest. Score not, ye'll not be scored.
And guess ye what? I have here, in my gourd,
A draught of wine, ripe juices of the grape.
Glum as he is now, merry as an ape
This wine of mine will make him. Will he drink?
Upon my life he will, and never wink."

And truth it was, this Cook, without a word,
Set to and drank till he had drained the gourd.
What need of that? he'd had enough before;

But not while drop was left, would he restore
This horn well-blown, but when he did, he spoke
Such thanks as may be said by drunken folk.

Our Host nigh burst with laughter at the sight,
And sighed and wiped his eyes for pure delight,
And said, "Well, I perceive it's necessary,
Where'er we go, good drink with us to carry.
What needeth in this world more strifes befall?
Good wine's the doctor to appease them all.
O, Bacchus, Bacchus! blessèd be thy name,
That thus can'st turn our earnest into game.
Worship and thanks be to thy deity.
So on this head ye get no more from me.
Now, Manciple, tell on thy tale, I pray."

"Well, sir," quoth he, "give heed to what I say."

[The Manciple then spoke a fable old,
How crows went black, but Chaucer hath not told

Canterbury from Harbledown Hill

Whether or no there at the little town,
Right on the hilltop, called Bob-up-and-down, —
Because from thence only down hill once more
And once more up hill travelers go before
The towers of the great cathedral rise
Majestic and resplendent on their eyes —
This troop, as pilgrims then were wont to do,
Reined up and stooped to kiss St. Thomas' shoe,
A relic which, in times uncritical,
Supported by its fees a hospital;
Yet well we may believe our cavalcade,
Each man after his fashion, kissed and paid.]

Short was the story, but when it was ended,
The sun had in the west so far descended,
'Twas wellnigh four. Our Host, as ever he
Was wont to guide our merry company,
Said thus: "My lords, of tales we lack but one."
[Yet what, forsooth, had those five craftsmen done?
And the Knight's Yeoman had not borne his part,
Nor that poor Ploughman of the holy heart.]
"Fulfilled now is my sentence and decree;
I trow that we have heard from each degree.
Almost fulfilled is all mine ordinance.
I pray to God to give that man good chance
Who tells this last tale to us lustily.

"Sir Priest," quoth he, "a vicar may'st thou be,
Or what? We would thy reverence not misname.
Be thou whate'er thou art, spoil not our game,
For every man save thee his tale hath told.

Unpack thy wallet; show what it may hold.
That look of thine meseems betokening
Thou should'st knit up for us a mighty thing.
Tell us a fable quick, by—chickenbones!"

The Parson

The Parson answered him in solemn tones:
"Thou wilt not get a fable told by me,
For Paul, in writing unto Timothy,
Reproveth them that prize the truth at less
Than fables and such very wretchedness.
Why should I scatter chaff out of my fist
When I may sow good wheat? Now if you list
To hear of virtue and morality,
Of penitence and immortality,
And please to give me sober audience,
Gladly will I, in Christian reverence,
Promote your higher pleasure, as I can;
But bear in mind, I am a southern man;
I can't alliterate,—*rum*, *ram*, *ruf* by letter—

And rhyme, God wot, I hold but little better;
And therefore, if ye like what I propose,
I'll tell to you a merry tale in prose
To knit up all this mirth and make an end.
And Jesu, of His grace, the wit me send
To guide you all, through this our ride's last stage,
In that all-perfect, glorious pilgrimage
To the Jerusalem celestial;
So if ye give me leave, anon I shall
Begin upon my tale, wherefore I pray
Declare your minds; no better can I say.

"My sermon hath no dangerous doctrines new.
I speak it all under correction due
Of scholars. I'm not learned in points of text;
Fear not to be by heresies perplexed;
Of Holy Writ I take the gist; the rest
I leave unto the Church, which knoweth best."

On that assurance, we gave prompt assent.
It seemed but suitable, as now we went
On to the city, that a priest should bless
Our entering in with words of godliness;
And so we bade our grumbling Host beseech
The Parson, as he had proposed, to preach.

Courteously our Host addressed him for us all:
"Sir Parish Priest," quoth he, "fair you befall!
Say what ye list, and we will gladly hear."
Then added he: "'Tis well the town is near.
Spin out your sermon till we come to town,
But hasten, for the sun is going down.
Be edifying, since ye must exhort.
God shed His grace upon you! But be short."

[Yet passing long that sermon was; of this
Our earthly life it told, and endless bliss
Wherein, beyond all memory of annoy,
The saints rejoice in one another's joy;
Where man's dark body shineth as the sun,
Where the mortal immortality hath won,
Where no heart hungers more, but all abide
With fullness of God's presence satisfied.
This glad eternal kingdom men may buy
By poverty of spirit, feasts on high
By thirst below, glory by meekness, rest
By labor, and the life forever blest
By death of sin. While thus the Parson said,
The western sky, like martyr's blood, grew red.
And lingering light tipped with adoring fires
The dim cathedral's tracery of spires.]

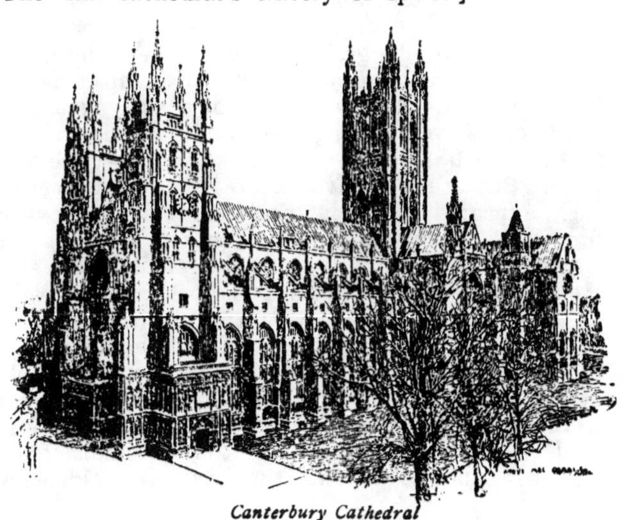

Canterbury Cathedral

APPENDIX

I

PILGRIMAGES

THE word pilgrim meant, at first, a wayfarer, but came in the Middle Ages to denote the traveler whose journey had a religious motive and goal. It is natural to wish to visit scenes connected with events of great interest to us, especially of sacred interest. The Jews from all over Palestine used to go up to worship at Jerusalem, their holy city, long before Christ was born. And it was hardly a hundred years after His death upon the cross that Christians began to come, sometimes from far away, to kneel upon Mount Calvary and pray to Christ there on the very ground where He had suffered.

Early in the fourth century there came among the pilgrims one of the greatest ladies then living in all Europe—Helena, the mother of the Roman emperor. This first Christian emperor, known as Constantine the Great, gave a strange account of his conversion to the new faith. He said that once, when he was leading his army to give battle to a strong enemy, there appeared to him in the noonday sky a cross of fire, with the words shining beneath it: "*In hoc signo vinces.*" "In this sign, thou shalt conquer." He conquered and believed. His mother then became a Christian and, almost eighty though she was, made the pilgrimage to Palestine. Here she discovered, or thought that she discovered, the site of the Holy Sepulcher, the cave in which Christ was born at Bethlehem, and even the true cross on which He died. She built churches over the sacred places,—churches that soon were thronged with kneeling pilgrims.

Helena's discoveries brought Christians in such multitudes all that costly, weary, perilous way to the Holy Land that a wise bishop tried to check the tide of pilgrimage. "Change of place," he said, "brings God no nearer. Where thou art, God will come to thee, if the dwelling of the soul is prepared for Him." But still the pilgrim hosts surged eastward, especially when the first thousand years since the birth of Christ had almost passed. Many people supposed that the end of the thousand years would bring the end of the world, and forsook business, homes, and families in a panic eagerness to reach Jerusalem before the Day of Judgment. "A multitude such as no one could have anticipated," wrote a man who was living in those times, "began to flow from all quarters toward the Saviour's tomb: first the lower class of people; then those of middle station; afterwards a number of the foremost kings and counts. Finally, and this had never happened before, many women of noble rank, together with those of a poorer class, proceeded thither. Some hoped death might find them there."

In the eleventh century Palestine, which had long since passed from the Romans to the Mohammedans, fell under the rule of a fierce race of Turks who robbed, enslaved, or slew the Christian pilgrims. From this state of things came to pass, one after another, the nine crusades, wars in which millions of Europeans, each wearing the badge of a blood-red cross, strove to rescue the Holy Sepulcher from the Saracens. The crusades, which, terrible as they were, had something beautiful at the heart of them, ended only a hundred years before the times described in Chaucer's book,—his own times, when pilgrimages even to the Holy Land were no longer heroic. In his day comparatively few English pilgrims went so far. Some visited the shrine of St. Peter at Rome and some the still nearer shrine of St. James in Spain, from which they would come home with their capes studded over with cockleshells, but many were easily satisfied with holiday jaunts to the healing wells of St. Mary of Walsingham, in Norfolk, or to the glorious church of St. Thomas of Canterbury, in Kent.

II

ST. THOMAS OF CANTERBURY

Thomas à Becket lived in the twelfth century. He was born in London during the reign of Henry I, the youngest son of William the Conqueror. This William had come from Normandy and, crossing the Channel with a great army, had invaded England. In the battle of Hastings, 1066, Harold, the native king, had perished, and William had seized the realm by the strong hand. To his French followers he gave the English lands and castles, the high places in church and state, while the Saxon nobles, so many as had not fallen on the field, fled from their homes to live like outlaws in fen and forest, or made what terms they could with the Conqueror. During the reigns of his sons, too, Normans were in favor, and needy Frenchmen flocked to England as to a shore of gold. The parents of Thomas à Becket were among these Norman immigrants. They settled in London, where Gilbert Becket seems to have made for himself an honorable place as a merchant citizen. Their son Thomas, born about 1118, was carefully reared by his mother,—a woman so charitable and so devout that she used to keep her boy's birthday by weighing him against an amount of money, food, and clothes, which she would give to the poor. At the age of ten, he was sent away to a school kept by monks at Merton, a few miles south of London. But soon his parents must have him home again and his education was continued at one of the three great London schools, where the boys learned Latin and logic, held public discussions and declamations and, in the outlying fields, played mighty football games, which all the city thronged to see. Thomas, though the son of a burgher, had made friends among the young nobles, and was as high-spirited and dashing as the best of them. He went to the University of Paris for his final theological studies, and came home fitted for a clerical career, but bearing himself like a Norman gallant. "He was now two and twenty years of age," says an old chronicler, "slim of growth and pale of hue, dark of hair, with a long nose and straightly-featured face; blithe of countenance was he, winning and lovable in all conversation, frank of speech in his discourse, but slightly stuttering in his talk, so keen of discernment and understanding that he could always make difficult questions plain after a wise manner."

Thomas returned to a saddened and impoverished home. His mother had died and his father had lost money through a series of fires that raged among the thatched and timbered houses of that old-time London, so that the student looked about for employment. His ability to read and write Latin, the language of official documents, secured him a position in the service of the city magistrates, where he gained a knowledge of practical politics. Then came an opportunity to enter the household of the Archbishop of Canterbury, Theobald, a great moral leader, who took him into such favor that the keen young Londoner presently became the close confidant and principal agent of the head of the English Church.

Theobald had set his hand to a difficult and dangerous work. He had undertaken to restore the realm of England, distressed by civil war and the misrule of the barons, to the control of a strong sovereign. While Thomas was still a London school-boy, Henry I had died, leaving no son, and the succession of his daughter, Matilda, was disputed by his nephew, Stephen. Grandson and granddaughter of the Conqueror, these two wrangled for the throne, staining the fields of England with blood and abandoning the helpless people to the greed and tyranny of their feudal lords. Theobald and Thomas worked neither for Matilda nor Stephen, but for a more royal soul than either, the son of Matilda and of Geoffrey of Anjou. This youth, Henry II, the first Plantagenet, was crowned in 1154, and from the outset treated Thomas à Becket as his familiar friend.

The square-built, rough-mannered young king, only twenty-one on his accession, admired and loved this all-accomplished commoner, whom he made Lord Chancellor of England, and loaded with honors. Now Becket lived with a magnificence that rivaled the royal court, and it was one of the king's rude jests to come clattering on horseback into his chancellor's banquet-hall and vault over the table to seat himself by Becket's side and eat a better dinner than was served in his own palace. People said that there were never two such friends in Christendom. Although the chancellor was the elder by some fifteen years, he was expert in feats of chivalry and had as fresh a zest as any lad for hunting and hawking, for wine and delicate fare, for mirth and revelry. He lived the life of the world with such grace and splendor proving himself on occasion a valiant soldier no less than an able statesman, that when, on the death of Theobald, in 1162, Henry appointed Becket to the archbishopric of Canterbury, it seemed that the choice could hardly have fallen on a more unpriestly personage. Thomas himself glanced down at his gay court suit and laughed at the idea of his being set over the dull-gowned Canterbury monks.

But Henry persisted. He had, as he thought, good reason for this selection. Becket, as chancellor, had shown himself steadfast and resourceful in supporting his sovereign, whose iron will and sturdy sense of justice were enlisted in the effort to bring that turbulent kingdom into order, against the barons. The king's feudal reforms were now well under way, and he was turning his attention to the church. He felt, and rightly, that all Englishmen should be equal before the law, yet the clergy, including readers and choristers as well as priests, could not be brought before the civil courts. Even though their crimes were capital, they could be judged only by the ecclesiastical courts, whose penalties were of the lightest. The clergy, however, stood stiffly for their ancient privileges, and Henry depended upon Thomas, once at the head of the English church, to bend it to the royal will.

But after all those years of affectionate intimacy, Henry did not know his man. As Archbishop of Canterbury, the luxurious worldling was suddenly transformed into an austere priest, who would not yield one jot of "the honor of his order." A terrible quarrel broke out between the former friends. Becket defied the royal commands, thwarted the royal purposes, and was forced to flee from England. It was six years before the pope was able to bring Henry to even a show of submission, and the archbishop was not without forebodings as he returned to Canterbury, where he was received with ringing of bells and every sign of welcome. But an outbreak of angry words from the king was enough to send four fierce barons spurring to the town. As these assassins, sheathed in mail and brandishing naked swords, burst from the cloisters into the northwest transept of the cathedral, the flock of monks, assembled for vespers, scattered from before them like barnyard fowl under a swoop of hawks. Only three were men enough to stand by their archbishop to the end, one of these, good to remember, being his old Merton schoolmaster. It was the early twilight of a winter day—December 29, 1170—and Becket in the shadows might have saved himself by flight, for there were many hiding-places in roof and crypt, but the archbishop faced his murderers like a knight, replying to their threats and taunts with flings of fearless scorn until their rain of blows had beaten him to death upon the pavement.

Becket dead was mightier than Becket living. The murdered archbishop, for whom the king, remembering the years of their friendship, made bitter mourning, was sainted by the Church as a holy martyr, miracles were wrought at his tomb, and his shrine became so splendid with the gifts of pilgrims that, when Erasmus visited it shortly after the time of Chaucer, "gold was the meanest thing to be seen."

III

GEOFFREY CHAUCER

More than two hundred years after the birth of Becket there was born, probably in London, the most famous pilgrim to his shrine, Geoffrey Chaucer. The date of his birth is not certainly known, but was most likely 1340 or thereabouts. The Plantagenets still wore the crown of England. Henry II had been succeeded by his sons Richard the Lion-Heart and John. The son of John, Henry III, had reigned in turn, and had been followed by his son, Edward I, whose own son, Edward II, had been deposed for his weak and selfish rule. In 1327 the son of Edward II, Edward III, then a lad of fourteen years, came to the throne, which he occupied for half a century. This was the king of Chaucer's youth and early manhood.

Like Becket, Chaucer was the son of a London merchant, who may have been of Norman descent. But the two hundred years had done much to mingle the strains of Norman and Saxon blood in England.

The French language, although still the tongue of fashion, was losing its hold on the law courts and the schools. The mass of the English people had risen from the sorry estate in which the Norman conquest left them to a fair degree of freedom and prosperity. Under the English banner, Norman knights and Saxon archers had fought side by side against the French, so that a sense of national unity had grown up. The subjects of Edward III thought of themselves and of one another as Englishmen.

The London of Chaucer's day was but a little city, as cities are reckoned now, a

> "London small, and white, and clean,
> The clear Thames bordered by its gardens
> green."

On the river street and hard by London bridge stood the wine-shop of John Chaucer, a thriving citizen who, in one way or another, had influence enough to obtain for his son a position in the household of Princess Elizabeth, wife of Lionel, third son of the king. Through two stray pages of an old account book we catch a glimpse of Chaucer at seventeen, a court dandy in red and black breeches, with a short cloak thrown over one shoulder and a few pieces of silver jingling merrily in the wallet hanging from his belt.

Two years later we hear again of Chaucer as having joined that magnificent and costly army which, in the autumn of 1359, Edward III led into France, the French king being already his prisoner in London. Among the many disasters which befell that splendid host, famine and disease proving more fatal enemies than the chivalry of France, King Edward doubtless reckoned it a trifling item in the sum total of his losses that Geoffrey Chaucer was taken prisoner in Brittany. But the young soldier was soon released, his monarch himself contributing sixteen pounds, nearly one thousand dollars in money value to-day, toward his ransom. After seven years Chaucer reappears in the records as Valet of the King's Chamber. This was a position held only by gentlemen. Its duties were light and, being performed for a king, would not be considered menial, although they comprised making beds, holding torches, going on errands, hanging the walls with tapestry, and doing whatever else the chamberlain might bid. Several of these valets attended their sovereign in his chamber, taking their meals there in his presence. "And each of them," says the old manuscript, "shall have for living a certain weight of bread, one gallon of beer, a mess of meat from the kitchen and yearly a robe in cloth or a mark in money,—and for shoes a certain sum at two seasons in the year."

But Chaucer served the king in the capacity of esquire also, for in a schedule of members of the royal household for whom Christmas robes were to be provided his name stands the seventeenth among those of thirty-seven esquires. These were of various sorts. There were Squires of the Mouth, whose duty it was to carve for the king, bear his cup, and taste his food, as a precaution against poison. There were Squires of the Body, who dressed and undressed the king, watched him in turn by day and by night, and anticipated all his wants. But probably Chaucer was one of the Squires of the Household, twenty of whom always attended the king whenever he stirred abroad. It was a part of their duty too, to bring the king's viands from the table where they were first tasted by the Squires of the Mouth to the royal banquet-board. We can imagine the young courtier, with that shy, "elfish," engaging face of his, dressed in the king's livery and carrying the covered silver dishes across the rush-strewn hall, having first quietly slipped bits of bread between his hands and the hot metal. We can see him riding out in the king's retinue or dining in the royal chamber with some score of other merry young gentlemen, their mirth a little hushed under the severe eye of the chamberlain. We can picture him, in the long winter evenings, withdrawing with the rest to the open halls of the palace, where it was the business of these esquires to be as sociable and entertaining as they could,—"to keep honest company after their cunning, in talking of chronicles of kings and of other policies, or in piping or harping,"—or singing of songs—"to help to occupy the Court and accompany strangers, till the time require of departing." And when the time required of departing, Geoffrey Chaucer and that one of his fellow-squires whose good fortune it was to be the poet's chum would go up to their bedroom, carrying each his own half-gallon of ale for comfort, his two Paris candles for light, and his fagot of cut wood for warmth, since their little chamber, which had for window a square opening closed by a wooden shutter, was cold and draughty enough. And then, while the other squire lounged on the "fair joined frame of oak," the pitcher of ale by his side, and presently drank himself drowsy, perhaps Chaucer busied himself with translations of French verses or with the shaping of delicate, fresh-hearted poems of his own after the French style, until he, too, fell sleepy, and lay down beside his comrade in their corded trundle-bed.

Chaucer married, perhaps as early as 1366, a lady named Philippa, "one of the damoiselles of the Queen's chamber." It is possible that this was Philippa Roet, whose sister Katharine became the wife of John of Gaunt, Duke of Lancaster, fourth son of the king and for many years the most powerful noble of the realm. If this be so, it would account for the court favor Chaucer seems to have enjoyed in middle life and for the various offices and dignities conferred upon him by the Crown. Seven times we find him sent on diplomatic missions, three of these to Italy, where he became acquainted with the new Italian literature. From that time forth his own poetry took on Italian themes and measures. The dainty grace of his early lyrics broadened and deepened into richer beauty. But the poet was also an active man of business. In 1374 he was appointed to a position in the custom-house,—a position which required him to inspect in person the cargoes of wools, skins, and tanned hides loaded and unloaded in the port of London and to keep the records in his own handwriting. Chaucer's task was no light one, for the wool trade was the most important of the kingdom. After one of these busy days, when at last his work was done and his accounts made up, the poet, who was a lifelong student, would return to his home—rooms in the city wall above one of the great stone gates—and would pore over some precious manuscript until his look was all dazed, so that his friends accused him of living like a hermit.

During these years Chaucer was the recipient of a pitcher of wine daily from the royal butler, the holder of a life-lease of his dwelling house, pensioner on the bounty of the king, and guardian over the lands and person of a young gentleman of fortune. In course of time he was privileged to do the work of the Customs by a clerk and no longer in person. It seems likely enough that he went on the Canterbury pilgrimage in April, 1385, the spring after his release from the daily drudgery of the custom-house.

Meanwhile the brilliant reign of Edward III had closed in loss, sorrow, and dishonor. His eldest son, the Black Prince, pride and hope of the nation, died in 1376, worn out by fruitless campaigns in France and Spain. The third son, Lionel, had died eight years earlier, and the second son did not outlive infancy. The fourth son, John of Gaunt, was the actual ruler of England during the dotage of his father, who died the year after the Black Prince.

The only son of the Black Prince, Richard II, a child of eleven years, succeeded to the throne, but his uncle still held the power. The great duke had rivals, however, especially his younger brother, the Duke of Gloucester, and in 1386 he was driven from the kingdom. Chaucer, like other friends and dependants of John of Gaunt, was made to feel the disgrace of his patron. The poet, who that autumn sat in Parliament as one of the members for Kent, suddenly found himself turned out of the custom-house altogether. It was one thing to give up the work and quite another to be deprived of the salary.

From this year of misfortune, too, there ceases in the state records all mention of his wife, whose name up to date had frequently occurred in the royal accounts, noting her as the recipient of gifts or pensions. It is probable that she died at about this time. For two years or more the poet was face to face with poverty. But in 1389 the "rose-red" Richard, impetuous and wayward, dismissed his council and assumed the charge of government himself, shaking off the control of the Duke of Gloucester and recalling the Duke of Lancaster to England. With the return of John of Gaunt, Chaucer's star swiftly rose again. He was appointed overseer of certain public buildings and made one of a commission for the repair of roads along the Thames. But presently he fell into need, notwithstanding a new pension from the Crown. He had to borrow money and was in danger of arrest for debt. In 1399 Henry Bolingbroke, son of John of Gaunt, supplanted his cousin on the throne, and made it one of his first cares of kingship to double the pension of his father's friend. In the following year, on the twenty-fifth of October, Chaucer died. He was buried in Westminster Abbey, in what is now known as Poets' Corner, for so many of England's bards lie there about him that, as was said long ago, it is "enough almost to make passengers' feet move metrically who go over the place where so much poetical dust is interred.''

It was a busy, varied life that this first of the great English poets led. He loved to read and he loved to murmur over the new music of his rhymes, fusing the Norman and Saxon into one enduring English speech. Better yet he loved, on a May morning, to slip out into the fields and watch the daisy open to the sun,—

> ''Kneling alwey, til hit unclosed was,
> Upon the smalĕ softë swotë gras.''

But he had to live in camps and courts, to journey by sea and land, and, more and more, as life went on, he had to work for his daily bread among plain English folk, merchants and sailors and carpenters, who helped him write better poetry than he had written before. For he learned the sweetness of patience and of charity,—how to season life with laughter and make the most of human fellowship. His heart had its sorrows, his mind had its grave thoughts of truth and righteousness, but as the world went harder and harder with him, he entered more and more into the secret of joy, so that in after times one who loved him well, Edmund Spenser, found something holy in this wise, twinkling, tender mirth of the old poet and hailed him as

> ''Most sacred happy spirit.''

www.ingramcontent.com/pod-product-compliance
Lightning Source LLC
LaVergne TN
LVHW020232110826
845151LV00003B/898

* 9 7 8 1 4 2 5 5 2 9 6 8 0 *